Heartfelt Hospitality

Radical & Rewarding

Jane Loerop

Copyright © 2013 Jane Loerop

All rights reserved.

ISBN: 1492283878

ISBN 13: 9781492283874

Library of Congress Control Number: 2013904984

CreateSpace Independent Publishing Platform

North Charleston, South Carolina

Contents

Acknowledgments vii

Foreword xi

Introduction xv

Chapter One: Starting Young, Starting Small 1

Chapter Two: Laying the Foundation 9

Chapter Three: Facing Our Fears 19

Chapter Four: Don't Do It Alone 29

Chapter Five: Facing Failure 39

Chapter Six: Joe from Skid Row 47

Chapter Seven: Dealing with Self-Destruction 55

Chapter Eight: Divine Interruptions 63

Chapter Nine: God, Where Is My Sister? 73

Chapter Ten: A Little Lamb 81

Chapter Eleven: Baby at Her Doorstep 89

Chapter Twelve: Spiritual Warfare 95

Chapter Thirteen: The Sting of Betrayal 115

Chapter Fourteen: A Desperate Call 121

Chapter Fifteen: The Next Step 129

Conclusion 139

Endnotes 143

Brief Description

Heartfelt Hospitality will stretch your soul, reveal hidden sins of selfishness in your heart, challenge your faith, and bring to life the deep secrets of agape love. If we are to be true to Jesus and his calling in our lives, we will step up to the challenge with faith and say: "Here am I; use me."

Heartfelt hospitality has little to do with manners and setting the table. It's far more than rules found in etiquette books. For author Jane Loerop, hospitality centers on welcoming those in need into your home and into your heart, sharing your unique spiritual gifts and the light of Jesus Christ. *Heartfelt Hospitality*, her deeply reflective new book, shares a lifetime of ministry doing just that, with the goal of inspiring others who seek to make a difference in the world by being caring and compassionate.

Whether around the world or on the next block, the opportunities in our lives to help the truly needy abound, as illustrated in this powerful, moving, spiritual resource. From her forays as a teenager ministering to a Kalamazoo family and reading Scripture to the children, Loerop sensed the Holy Spirit touch her heart. Thus began a forty-year journey that guided her and her husband, Ken, through caring for the less fortunate, both nearby and in far-flung countries, such as the Dominican Republic and the Ukraine. Welcoming a wide range of individuals into their home, including taking in one young man as part of their family, the author and her husband have learned all aspects of ministry.

Each chapter of *Heartfelt Hospitality* shares a real-life story of salvation, spirituality, and sometimes the trials that can rattle one's faith. The chapters include meditation and questions that can be used for personal reflection or group discussions. Often the tales uplift, such as her recollection of a homeless Alabama family who became an integral part of her church community, or her work with Little Lambs and single mothers. Other times they mine the darker implications of taking risks on behalf of God, including her work with an irresponsible family who met a tragic end at the hands of an ex-husband.

All the while, Loerop has learned that a deep faith in God is guidance in finding the best path to truly help those who can most benefit from the support. With sensitivity and abiding love and belief, each story demonstrates the potential that everyone has when one taps into his or her spiritual talents and finds an inroad to minister. *Heartfelt Hospitality* demonstrates how, with love and caring, we can all be doers of the will of God and enfold others into our lives in a way that is meaningful and deeply moving.

Acknowledgements

Throughout my life, people have said to me, "Jane, you need to write a book." I never took them seriously because I was too busy with my family and ministry work. It wasn't until I had contact with Elaine Beck, whom I hadn't seen for thirty years, that I thought more seriously about writing a book. Ken and I were in Florida, and we called home to check our messages. There was a message that Elaine left requesting that we return the call. I returned her call, and she was crying uncontrollably and said, "My son was just shot." I told her that we were in Florida, and we could meet her in Alabama. We agreed to meet at Wal-Mart not too far from where she lived. As we were traveling to Alabama, I felt a prompting from the Lord to write this book.

I thought of all of the other families we have helped along life's path and my desire to reconnect with them. These individuals impacted the lives of my husband and me forever. Maybe others can benefit from what they have taught us: the blessing of showing hospitality and taking up God's challenge to literally enfold others into one's family. We have reaped the blessings as a result.

I am grateful to my mother, who set the example of heartfelt hospitality in loving people along life's path. She set the bar very high for her children to follow. She always loved to entertain and serve delicious dinners, and she decorated the table with fresh flowers and gold silverware on a lace tablecloth. It was always set this way, whether she was having a neighbor in for coffee or relatives over for a formal Sunday dinner.

An example of my mother's authentic hospitality that touched my heart the most was when she invited twenty ladies over from the mental health hospital in Kalamazoo, Michigan, along with their nurses. She showed them the same genuine beauty in entertaining as she did to everyone else who entered her home.

My husband's gift of mercy and generosity to the needy made the gift of authentic hospitality possible for me to put into practice. Ken allowed me to open the door to the hungry, the homeless, those in crisis, and the orphans. He never knew who would be at the dinner table. This was true not only on Sundays but throughout the week. Yet he rarely complained or said "No." At times he kept me in balance, but he was always open to the next challenge that God sent our way.

Our children were flexible in welcoming the next person or family that God brought into our life. They grew up in a multiracial home due to the members of many races who sat with us at our kitchen table and with whom we shared our lives. Now they are married and have families of their own. They are duplicating genuine hospitality in different ways but with the same theme. Even our grandchildren are getting involved in ministering to orphans in other countries.

Yes, I needed to take up the challenge of writing this book, no matter what the effort or the cost might be. It is not for my benefit but to bring glory to God and to encourage others to take a leap of faith.

Without my friend Robert Greer, who served as my editor and book collaborator, we never would have finished this mission into a world that says, "Just say *yes* to God."

We have been blessed—*to be a blessing*.
We have been loved—*to bring love*.
We have been taught the message—*to teach others*.
We have been changed—*to help bring change in others' lives*.

Bob Greer: Editor and Collaborator

Bob Greer: Editor and Collaborator
Master of Arts in Theological Studies,
Wheaton College
Ph. D in Systemic Theology, Marquette University

At the request of the author, all royalties will
be given to Single Mothers and orphans at the
Little Lambs Ministry in the Ukraine.

Foreword

by Hope Gaffner, Granddaughter

The person who has had the biggest influence in my life lives in Elmhurst, Illinois. She is seventy-one years old, and she has had an impact on more people's lives than I could imagine influencing. Throughout her life, she has been involved in many service projects. She led a preschool ministry for kids at her church. This not only brought many people into the church who would not normally attend a church but also provided two hours of childcare for working parents. Through this she was able to share Christ's love with many people.

She is my grandmother!

Every time I enter her home, she has somehow found a new way to share the light of Jesus with others. She loves inviting people to her home who don't have families with whom to spend Thanksgiving. Sometimes surprises come and people show up whom she doesn't even know. This past Thanksgiving, four families, whom none of us recognized, came to her house and started eating with us. My grandma had no idea who they were, but she made sure they felt welcome. Recently, she started a ministry for single mothers who are struggling. Through this she is able to reach out to hurting women. The stories go on and across the world.

Not only does she serve locally, but she also serves in the Ukraine. She has now been on fourteen mission trips to the Ukraine, showing love to orphans. Two years ago, I joined her on one of her annual trips. At first, I was not sure if I could do it. After all, three weeks is a long time to be away from the comforts of home. After much consideration, however, I decided to go. In June 2010, my grandma and I boarded a plane for an eleven-hour flight to the Ukraine. As I traveled there, I had no idea what to expect.

When we arrived, we split into groups, and I was placed with the group who cared for the nine- to eleven-year-olds. Each day, my love for those children grew. It broke my heart to see what they had to live through. I saw constant physical abuse from both the teachers at the orphanage and the other children. I tasted the unappetizing food they had to eat. I heard numerous stories of horrible things those children experienced.

Then my grandmother had an overstressed tendon in her heel, but she didn't let her struggles keep her from serving. Every day she would get up and do everything she could to show the orphans that she cared about them, even if it meant limping by the end of the day.

Reflecting on this trip, it was hard for me to come back and live in the United States with everything we have, knowing there are so many people around this world who have so little. The more I see how my grandma lives and how many different people she has blessed, the more I want my life to become like hers. She has shown me what our purpose in life really should be about: caring for others. I don't want to simply live a "normal" life, living in a house bigger than I need and spending more money on clothes and food than millions of people around the world will ever have. With this focus, I have decided to pursue a career in nursing. My goal is to change people's lives both here in the United States and in Third World countries.

This year is my grandparents' fiftieth wedding anniversary, and they thought a good way to celebrate would be to bring our family—children and grandchildren—on a three-generational mission trip. They purchased twenty-three tickets, and we went together on a life-changing mission trip to the Dominican Republic. We fed a meal to people in the poorest village I have ever seen. We painted a school. We assisted in building a home for a family of seven whose house was burned down a year ago. And we showed God's love to many Dominicans.

Through these experiences and the ones yet to come, I hope to encourage others to also demonstrate the same spirit of caring that my grandma has shown. In addition, I hope to continue to make a difference in people's lives and fulfill God's calling in James 1:27: "Religion that God our Father accepts as pure and faultless is this: to look after orphans and widows in their distress and to keep oneself from being polluted by the world."

Grandma has taught me that when I see hurting people and horrible situations, I shouldn't expect things to change on their own. I need to be the one to push for change. Without my grandma being such a role model and pushing me past my comfort zone to step inside others' lives, I believe what I would have done in my life and what I hope to do would look completely different.

Introduction

This book is for the ordinary person who wants to make a difference in the world by being caring and compassionate. Each chapter is centered on a particular story. As you read, ask yourself: "Where would I fit into these stories? Who are the needy in my world?" You will probably come up with many more ideas beyond what my family experienced. I would love to hear from you, and together we can enlarge upon this small start of engaging hospitality. Then may we multiply a hundredfold our ideas for reaching out to the needy (http://radicalhospitalityjaneloerop.blogspot.com).

You will find the word *hospitality* referred to as *authentic*, *biblical*, and *radical*. They mean the same thing, because biblical hospitality is both authentic and radical.

The rewards of biblical hospitality are great. I yearn for Christians everywhere to put this ministry into their daily practice.

> Heartfelt Hospitality changes peoples' lives so they no longer think in terms of *me, myself, my schedule*. If more people engaged in authentic hospitality across the globe, the chain reaction would change the many generations that follow.

In this book, I will share some of our experiences with you. You will learn:
- what happens when a thirteen-year-old joins a family of five children;

- how God touches lives after we delivered Christmas gifts to the needy for thirty years;
- what happens after pouring five years of love, finances, and spiritual direction into a family of seven;
- whether we faced success or failure when an ex-con and his family chose to live with us when he was released from prison;
- what happened after I picked up an abused pregnant woman; and
- how my one and only sister came as a refugee from Vietnam.

We all struggle with the fact that it's much easier to be a reader and not a doer of the will of God. How do we change this? What does God expect of us? Christian leaders can motivate Christians to do almost anything except practice biblical hospitality, because, more than almost anything else, biblical hospitality stretches us. It takes us way out of our comfort zones and interrupts our daily routines and even our privacy.

Does biblical hospitality guarantee church growth? No. That is, it doesn't guarantee church growth if you think of it in terms of numbers and increasing church attendance. But it does bring about church growth if you think of it in terms of growing individuals toward spiritual maturity. That is a certainty: biblical hospitality will cause us to grow in love and obedience. Authentic hospitality is welcoming people regardless of what baggage might be in their lives. It is indiscriminately accepting a person and saying to him or her: "You matter to God." It is seeing people from the inside instead of focusing on their outward appearance. It is seeing a soul that is destined for heaven.

Why, then, don't more Christians engage in this ministry? Could it be that this ministry is so foreign to them that it is impossible for them to wrap their minds around it? Could it be, I wonder, that Christians don't know how to get started, that they don't have a good idea of what this ministry actually looks like, that they are not rightly acquainted with its peculiar struggles and blessings? Perhaps they believe that this is simply not their spiritual gift. I hope that once you are finished reading this book, these questions will be answered for you and you will begin to see your role in this important ministry.

I am no different from any of you. I am merely a little blonde lady who has a heart for the hurting people of the world. If God can use me, God can use anybody. We all take different paths, and we are all used by God in different ways. But we are all called by God to share his love in this world.

As I already mentioned, each chapter is centered on a story from my life as I reached out to someone (or a group of people) with God's love. This book, then, is not filled with many persuasive arguments and theories. Other books do that much better than I will ever be able to do. Rather, this is a book full of real-life examples. Heartfelt hospitality, I firmly believe, is more caught than taught.

The Apostle Paul made this same point when he said: "Join with others in following my example, and take note of those who live according to the pattern God gave us" (Phil. 3:17). I believe that Christians need examples—scores of examples, one after another—of how this ministry plays itself out in the real world. This book follows in that tradition.

One more thing: When I say *hospitality*, I do not mean something out of Emily Post or Martha Stewart, or a fancy get-together where we show off our latest silverware or prepare a delicious new dessert, fancy salad, or marinated steak. I'm talking about meeting the needs of the truly needy, who live nearby, who are in our neighborhoods, or, for one reason or another, have crossed our paths.

For the longest time, we have left that kind of hospitality to rescue missions or some secular social agency. "Let them take care of those people," many Christians have said. Those days, I believe, are coming to an end. God is calling Christians to become more directly involved in this vital ministry.

Today needy people are not just on skid row. Many are within our churches. How many of us have heard our pastors, while leading prayer on Sunday mornings, ask God to care for those in our congregations who are either unemployed, under-employed, or something similar? Are not these kinds of petitions becoming increasingly common? How many of us are aware of people in the communities where we live, perhaps not even Christians, who are struggling with similar concerns? Many of us, I believe, know of such people. They are all around us.

If you need further convincing, listen to the words of Jesus: "When you give a luncheon or dinner, do not invite your friends, your brothers or sisters, your relatives, or your rich neighbors; if you do, they may invite you back and so you will be repaid. But when you give a banquet, invite the poor, the crippled, the lame, the blind, and you will be blessed. Although they cannot repay you, you will be repaid at the resurrection of the righteous" (Luke 14:12–14).

What a wonderful picture this presents of what our table should look like. May it start in your home within the next few months. Invite widows, single parents, jobless, homeless, abused, handicapped, and those different from you in appearance and beliefs.

In the first-century church, the purpose of hospitality was to provide people with food, clothing, and shelter. What is more, throughout the New Testament, the church was instructed to give high priority to this ministry. Let's look at some more verses in the New Testament:

"Share with God's people who are in need. Practice hospitality" (Romans 12:13).

"Now the overseer must be above reproach, the husband of but one wife, temperate, self-controlled, respectable, hospitable, able to teach" (1 Timothy 3:2).

"Offer hospitality to one another without grumbling" (1 Peter 4:9).

"We ought therefore to show hospitality to such people so that we may work together for the truth" (3 John 8)

> **MEDITATION**
> Beginning a ministry of heartfelt hospitality requires rethinking what it means to be a Christian. The cost is high, but the rewards are abundant.

QUESTIONS FOR PERSONAL REFLECTION OR GROUP DISCUSSION

1. How would you define hospitality? What would you add to complete the definition stated by the author?

2. What is the first step you have taken or hope to take toward hospitality in your community?

3. Have you prayed about what your spiritual gifts might be?

4. Are you using your gifts? How are your gifts impacting the people who God puts in your path?

5. Which guests sit at your table for lunch or dinner, outside of family or a small group from church?

6. Is it OK with you that this group of people might never invite you to their own homes?

7. What are you or your church doing for the unemployed, homeless, and needy in your community?

Chapter One

STARTING YOUNG, STARTING SMALL

My childhood memories take me back to Kalamazoo, Michigan, a moderately sized city situated in the Midwest and surrounded by paper mills, farmland, lakes, and rivers. My family attended a conservative church. It provided spiritual guidance for my life that I could put into practice as I matured.

Like most of my childhood friends, I could hardly wait to get my driver's license. On my sixteenth birthday, the day finally arrived. Now I could be like my boy cousins and have the freedom and mobility of driving a car. That day, however, was one of the worst snowstorms of that winter. Still, I insisted on getting my license. Not surprisingly, the Kalamazoo policeman was rather reluctant to take me out for a test drive. I reminded him that I was legally of age. He gave in, and we only went two miles for my driving test. I passed! What a thrill that was for me. My father gave me permission to drive the family car, a blue Impala Chevrolet convertible.

The following summer, I heard about a needy family who lived on the north side of Kalamazoo. I wrote down the address on a scrap piece of paper and tucked it in my pocket.

I let a few families at church know that a poor family needed some children's clothes. God blessed me with three bags of clothes, and I placed them in the backseat of the convertible. In those days there was no GPS; I just had the address on my scrap of paper. Fortunately, I knew the location of North Westnedge Ave., and I decided to follow the house numbers. By this time, I was outside of the city limits and in the celery farms. When I finally found the house, I pulled alongside the curb, paused, and looked it over. Paint was peeling off the outside walls. In place of a lawn was dirt mixed with weeds, and clutter was everywhere. The entire neighborhood was no different. Each house had the same basic appearance. The smell of ripening celery filled the air. If Kalamazoo had a ghetto where the poor lived, this was it.

I refused to be afraid or intimidated. I stepped out of the car, walked up to the front door, and knocked. A small child opened the door. His face was smudged with dirt, and his hair was unkempt. And, to my surprise, he was still in his underwear at two o'clock in the afternoon! Behind him stood six other children, all poorly dressed and dirty. The mother, who was quite overweight, walked up to the door and greeted me.

She looked me over and cautiously said, "Hello." I said, "You do not know me, but I have a love gift for you and your children."

I quickly went back to the car and brought my three large bags of clothes to the mother. I told her that I hoped some of the clothes might fit her children. The mother and her children seemed excited to receive the free clothes. As I shared a little about myself, I mentioned that my grandparents at one time owned a celery farm.

I then asked, "Can I return next week and share a Bible story with the children?"

"Yes," she replied, "I would like that." The children jumped up and down, excited that I was coming back. My heart was filled with joy. In less than fifteen minutes, this family had received my efforts with warmth.

Saying "Yes" to God

I remember years ago someone sharing with me a little saying about revival. Though I can't remember the exact words, it went something like this: *Revival begins with you.* It doesn't begin with your husband, your wife, your pastor, your congregation, or anyone else. It begins *with you.*

This is a hard lesson for many of us to learn. Many of us wish that revival would begin somewhere else so we can just tag along. But it doesn't work that way.

Anne Graham Lotz repeated this idea about revivals in her book *The Magnificent Obsession*. She wrote: "The revival we need now is not a tent meeting or a series of church services designed to save the lost. It's something completely different: authentic, personal revival."[1]

In *My Heart's Cry*, another of Lotz's books, she added: "About four years ago, God began to stir my heart with the desperate need for revival in the hearts of His people. However, the doors did not open at that time for me to do anything. Instead, God began to work in my personal life to bring me to a point of desperation for a fresh touch from Him."[2]

What was Anne's point? Revival begins small, with the individual, and at a moment in time when that individual senses the touch of the Holy Spirit upon his or her heart. Many of us are so distracted, however, that we miss the Holy Spirit. We don't feel the touch or hear the quiet voice. But when we do, and respond, as we should, revival has begun.

As a young girl of sixteen, I sensed the Holy Spirit touch my heart about ministering to a needy family. Following through and actually going to that house was a big step. Was I frightened? Did I have second thoughts? No, not really. As a child I had memorized Scripture verses, and they seemed to take away any thoughts of fear. "There is no fear in love, but perfect love casts out fear" (1 John 4:18). My love was far from perfect, but I knew the Lord was with me. That was all that really mattered. There are times when God gives us a childlike, trusting faith, and this was one of those moments for me.

It's hard to imagine saying no to the Lord of the universe, but we do it all too often. And we are the losers when we do. Life takes on eternal dimensions when we say yes.

The ministry of heartfelt hospitality begins when we say yes to God. What happens when we do this? We find ourselves radically obedient and radically blessed. In her book, *What Happens When Women Say Yes to God*, Lysa TerKeurst put it this way:

How tragic to miss God's divine appointments. I just kept wondering, How many times have I told you no, God? How many times because I was too tired, too insecure, too uncertain, too busy, or too selfish, have I walked right past your divine appointment for me and missed experiencing you? I lifted up my heart to the Lord and whispered, "Please forgive me for all those nos. Right now I say yes, Lord. I say yes to You before I even know what You might ask me to do. I simply want You to see a yes-heart in me.[3]

The next Sunday afternoon, as promised, I returned to this home on the north side of Kalamazoo alongside a ripening celery field. We then gathered in the front room of the house for Bible story time. The room had no furniture except for one chair. The mother sat in the chair. I sat on the floor with the seven children. They ranged from two to twelve years old.

The room was a sight. The walls and floor were dirty. The children were still unkempt. Their clothes were dirty. All their faces were smudged with dirt. Their hair was uncombed, and the room reeked of body odor.

I disciplined my mind to ignore the sights and smells. Instead, I kept my focus on the Lord, on the children's hearts, and on the Gospel of Jesus Christ. The Bible story that I chose to share with them was the Parable of the Lost Lamb from the Gospel of Luke. The children, I explained, were like lost sheep stuck in a briar bush struggling to get free from all of the thorns in the bush. Jesus was the Good Shepherd who was looking for the one lamb that was bleating. I shared with them that they were like that little lamb trying to get free, and they would be free from sin, those things that we do that make God unhappy, by inviting Jesus to live in their hearts as their Savior.

These children were hearing about Jesus for the first time. They listened well. That day seeds of the Gospel were sown in their hearts. They needed to be watered for many weeks.

Near the end of the summer, two of the children accepted Christ as their Lord and Savior. The angels in heaven rejoiced on that day!

Changing Attitudes

As the weeks went by, the mother and seven children became friendlier to me. They looked forward to the arrival of my blue Impala Chevrolet each Sunday afternoon.

At the young age of sixteen, I learned that the ministry of biblical hospitality was controversial (and it still is!). Rather than engaging the church directly, some think that we should send the poor and needy to rescue missions, orphanages, soup kitchens, and the like. Churches, people say, have standards that must be upheld—standards of cleanliness, orderliness, dress codes, and so on. In my young, idealistic mind, I had no idea that Christians thought this way. Thankfully, as I grew into adulthood, I learned that not all churches are like this.

The next step was to invite the family to church with me. I decided to bring them on a Sunday evening. To my surprise, however, one of my family members would not allow me to do this. His reason? He said that this family dressed poorly and had body odor. In our church, everyone came to church washed and in his or her Sunday best. The family from the north side of Kalamazoo simply would not fit in, and the whole church would be aghast. Therefore, I brought the church to them. For the rest of the summer, until I went to college in September, I visited this family every Sunday afternoon and told them stories from the Bible.

Heartfelt hospitality will stretch your soul, reveal hidden sins of selfishness in your own heart, challenge your faith, and bring to light the deep secrets of agape love. But if we are to be true to Jesus and his calling in our lives, we will step up to the challenge with faith and say: "Here am I; use me."

> **MEDITATION**
> *"Truly I tell you, whatever you did for one of the least of these brothers and sisters of mine, you did for me"* (Matthew 25:40).

QUESTIONS FOR PERSONAL REFLECTION OR GROUP DISCUSSION

1. In the Sermon on the Mount, Jesus said, "But seek first his kingdom and his righteousness, and all these things will be given to you as well" (Matt. 6:33). What does it mean to "seek first his kingdom"?

2. Note that there is no age bracket when one is led by the Holy Spirit to follow God. This is true if you are in grade school, a teen, or an adult. How do you know if the Holy Spirit is prompting you?

3. Brainstorm some ideas of "first-step" kinds of ministry related to heartfelt or radical hospitality. Try to come up with at least five ideas.

4. Most churches are typically prim and proper places where people come to worship God. Yet, because of this, the destitute and truly needy people feel out of place. What can be done to make all people feel more welcomed?

Chapter Two

LAYING THE FOUNDATION

During my teen years, I imagined that someday I would be serving God as a teacher. Children were and still are my passion. When I went to Calvin College in Grand Rapids, Michigan, I chose my subject courses to prepare me for the career of education.

At the end of my freshman year at Calvin, I met Ken. Through the summer break from school, we continued our relationship with letters and a few weekend visits. Ken returned to school for his sophomore year, and at the end of the year, he knew he wanted to pursue his life's vocation in Chicago.

Ken worked as a tool and die operator and envisioned making no more than five dollars an hour for the rest of his life. He therefore wondered if I could ever be happy being married to him and living with limited funds. When

I told him that I envisioned having six children, he was all the more concerned, since that meant six additional mouths to feed, six additional bodies to clothe, and so on. But I explained to him that money was not the focus of my life. When it came to money and lifestyle, I could accept whatever God brought my way.

Following my graduation from Calvin College with a BS degree in elementary education, we were married and moved to Bellwood, Illinois, one of the western suburbs of Chicago.

Marriage: The Big Picture

Many Christians who get married, I believe, miss the big picture of marriage.

> Though loving one another, having children, and companionship are all part of marriage, the bigger picture is this: it is an opportunity to work together as a team in the fulfillment of a divine mission in life.

This does not mean that both husband and wife should be involved in the same exact ministry, but marriage should principally have an outward rather than an inward focus. Keith A. Sherlin wrote:

> *One of the biggest problems today when couples marry is they have no divine mission in life. They marry for sensual pleasures, for financial reasons, for familial goals, or for other reasons without ever sensing and knowing a divine mission and purpose. God ordained the marriage unit as a team of two that will work to implement God's plan and rule*

> *over some area of life. A godly marriage will have a divine mission if it is rightly focused. The two will have a sense of destiny to accomplish God's plan in their respective areas of life. As a team they will set out on a divine journey.*[4]

It is this divine journey that keeps marriage fresh. Our personal fulfillment is found in God and in service to him. We are then free to love each other without the temptation of making too many demands of the other. Because our deepest fulfillment comes from God, we are free to accept one another as God created us. Most importantly, we do not expect the other to meet the deepest needs of our hearts.

Ours is not a perfect marriage, but Ken and I have worked at it and kept our commitment to each other. Ken had his business, and together we cared for the children. We strove to make service to God our principal objective.

We, of course, discipled our own children, and now our grandchildren. But it didn't stop there. We both have had ministries in the church we attend. But it didn't stop there, either. We have had outreach to our neighbors, friends, and whoever else God has brought along our path.

At times, our children felt shortchanged, that we did not devote enough time to them. I know, for example, that they wished we had attended more of their sporting activities. We were not the perfect parents, but God's grace covered our errors. At bedtime, I remember apologizing to them for not being as attentive to their needs as I should have been. In the long run, though, our adult children look back with thankfulness that our home was a place where serious ministry for God took place. And they are now duplicating that in their own households.

In Bellwood, Illinois, Ken continued to work as a tool and die operator. In time, he was promoted to tool designer and then to sales engineer. As time went by, he bought Drummond Industries with a partner.

All through these years, I yearned for an evangelistic outreach. I often asked myself: how will my community know that Christians live in this house? Every month, I made a decoration for my front door with a verse from the Bible on it. I hoped that it would communicate to at least a few people who came to my door that someone lived there who loved the Lord. In the wintertime, only the mail person, the delivery from the pharmacists, and the children that I tutored after school hours came to my door. Being a mom with children who were frequently ill, it was difficult to reach out to the community. But God used even those small efforts to make a difference in our little town. I was fulfilling my passion by being with our children and tutoring.

After eight years, we outgrew our two-bedroom home in Bellwood, since I was expecting our fourth child. We then moved further west to Elmhurst. Once again, I wondered how I could reach out to people in this new community. The thought came to my mind that I should pass out invitations to the ladies in the neighborhood to come over for coffee and fellowship. I put a note in everyone's mailbox in the radius of two blocks inviting women to my home. Five ladies showed up at ten o'clock on Thursday morning. Wow, God gave me my heart's desire. Now, where would I go from there?

After a few months, we decided to start a Bible study. Included in the group were two women, Carol and Chris.* We three became good friends. We prayed and studied the Bible together, and a close bond developed between us. Carol had no car, so I took her grocery shopping once a week. We continued this routine for the next twenty years. Chris suffered from cancer. She proved to be a role model for me, since she was always on the lookout for needy people to whom we could minister together. Our friendship deepened until the day she succumbed to her cancer and entered the presence of God.

CELEBRATING CHRISTMAS IN OUR NEW COMMUNITY

One year, just before Christmas, I learned of some needy families in our community through local agencies and through our preschool church ministry called "Little Lambs." We asked our children to empty their piggy banks. We converted their change into dollar bills at our local bank for the poor people we were going to visit. Ken and I purchased a number of gifts.

We then visited these families. With Ken dressed up as Santa, we crowded together on their front porch, rang their doorbells, and greeted them by singing, "We Wish You a Merry Christmas." Then we read the Christmas story and concluded with our children giving them one dollar and a Christmas gift. We told each family that the gifts were just symbolic of the gift that God gave to us on Christmas Day: his one and only son, Jesus. He sacrificed his life for our sins so that we could have eternal life with him. The gifts were just a reminder to these families that someone out in the community cared for them.

One of the families we visited, we will never forget because both parents were deaf. Knowing this ahead of time, we brought along a filmstrip projector and showed them the Christmas story on one of their walls. With hand motions, we told them that we loved them and would pray for them. As we returned to our station wagon and the children piled into the backseat,

I turned on the radio, and to our surprise, the station was playing Handel's "Hallelujah Chorus." The music touched our children, since they knew that those two deaf adults would never hear and enjoy this magnificent music that so profoundly praised our Savior and stirred our hearts.

REACTIONS FROM OUR CHILDREN

Mark, our youngest child, reflecting on our visits to the needy families, said, "I felt a little embarrassed and awkward since our family wasn't the most musically talented group. Still, we went up to the homes of strangers and sang carols. The families knew that there was someone in the community who loved them. As we left after sharing the good news of Christmas, we sensed a feeling of real joy." Mark also said, "Looking back to what we have done as family has made me more sensitive to the needs of the poor."

Steve, our second-oldest son, said, "This experience made me more generous in giving to the needy."

Debbie, our second daughter, said, "I realized how thankful I was as my eyes were opened to those who had fewer material possessions than we did."

Brad, our "adopted son," said, "This was really special because it wasn't done through an assigned organization. By word of mouth, from individuals we knew, we learned of those who had a need that we attempted to meet."

Recently, I was meeting with the steering committee of our single mothers support group, and a woman, Lori, inquired whether or not it was our family who came to her house thirty years ago. She said that the family who visited her house gave a crocheted vest to her and her sister. She described where she lived and gave the name of her mother. The gifts I did not recall, but I did remember the home and her mother and the children quite well. In fact, I even recalled her mother's first and last name. The good news is that Lori's mother surrendered her life to Christ before she died. Usually, we never met the families again after we gave them their gifts. But this was an affirmation to me that our efforts did make a difference decades later.

Discipling Our Own Children

If we think that raising our children in the ways of the Lord is having family devotions, sending them to Sunday school, and expecting them to sit quietly in church, we are missing the boat. It is much more than that. We need to involve them in family ministry. And with a hurting world all about us, what better way to do this but to reach out to the poor and needy and show them Christ's love?

This, I believe, is what God meant when he said the following words:

> *Hear, O Israel: The LORD our God, the LORD is one. Love the LORD your God with all your heart and with all your soul and with all your strength. These commandments that I give you today are to be upon your hearts. Impress them on your children. Talk about them when you sit at home and when you walk along the road, when you lie down and when you get up. Tie them as symbols on your hands and bind them on your foreheads. Write them on the doorframes of your houses and on your gates. (Deut. 6:4–9)*

I understand this passage to mean that parents are to disciple their children formally (in class) and informally (outside of class). And, rather than expecting others to do this for them—such as Sunday school teachers—the primary responsibility falls on parents.

Our oldest daughter, Mary, believes that her involvement in these outreach ministries when she was a child has had a profound effect on her spiritual life as an adult. She wrote:

> *God used those experiences to help me develop a heart of compassion for the people Christ loves. Jesus came to give of himself and provide healing in the many ways that sin has created pain, separation, and injustice in our lives. Through Jesus's love, God is glorified. We, by reflecting Christ's love to the people God sends our way, are glorifying and bringing light and healing to this hurting world.*
>
> *I've struggled with why we have been given so much and others so little. I have been challenged to see that joy is in Christ, not in material possessions. And I continue to try to understand and seek out what my part is in bringing compassion, mercy, justice, and love to others. I know that part of God's mission for me is to also help my children reflect Christ's love in their lives. This is what my parents have done, and this is a blessing that can be passed from generation to generation until Christ comes, and we can fully glorify God in the world of peace, joy, and love.*

Parents should remember that their children are watching them. Their understanding of the Christian faith comes first and foremost from Mom and Dad. If Mom and Dad treat Christianity like a hobby, so will they. If Mom and Dad's true priorities and interests lie elsewhere, theirs will too. Yet, if the parents emphasize serious Christian ministry in the home, sharing Christ's love with others, the likelihood is higher that the children will pick up on this and cultivate the same attitudes.

The idea of sharing gifts with the needy began thirty-five years ago with just one family. The desire to help others now has inspired the members of Elmhurst Christian Reformed Church (ECRC) and has touched the lives of hundreds of families throughout the past several years. It has proven to be a blessing to the Lord, to the church, to people in our local community, and now to people around the world.

This project recently has become known as "Glimmers of Hope" and gives families at ECRC an opportunity to purchase items listed on Christmas trees in our lobby for needy families or prisoners, clean water in a Third World country, and items for World Renew. World Renew is an organization sponsored by the Christian Reformed Denomination to help needy people throughout the world. I am sharing what we do to encourage you to apply a similar idea in your family or local church.

"Children are a heritage from the LORD, offspring a reward from him" (Ps. 127:3).

> **Meditation**
> When we think of biblical hospitality, we should not forget to include our children and spouses. As much as possible, it should be a family affair.

QUESTIONS FOR PERSONAL REFLECTION OR GROUP DISCUSSION

1. Many Christians getting married have no clear idea that marriage should be a divine journey where they are active in some well-defined ministry. When the notion of divine journey is well understood, what do husbands and wives tend to emphasize in their lives?

2. How are you communicating to your neighbors that you are a Christian family?

3. This chapter points out that a family ministry of biblical hospitality is feasible for many Christian homes. Reaching out during Christmas time and bringing cheer and some other tangible blessing to the poor in your neighborhood is one way of doing this. What would be some other ministry variations?

4. If parents limit the Christian training of their children to family devotions, faithful attendance in Sunday school, and making sure that the children sit quietly in church, they are missing the boat. Why is this true?

5. What can you do as an individual or family to include others during holidays and other special events, such as Thanksgiving, Fourth of July, block parties, and so on?

6. Christmas is the typical time of giving and exchanging gifts with one another. How can you engage your family to make this an experience that they will never forget?

Chapter Three

FACING OUR FEARS

"You have a home waiting for you in heaven," I told Pat. Pat looked back at me with tired eyes. Her breathing had become labored. If it weren't for the two tubes in her nostrils, she wouldn't be breathing at all. Her battle with lung cancer had been long and painful. We both knew the end was near. Cancer was claiming another—this time, my dear friend. Soon, perhaps within a day or two, she would leave this world and be transported by God's angels to her new home in glory.

"Yes," she replied, "a new home."

Though still looking into Pat's eyes, in my mind I thought of her thirteen-year-old son, Brad. Brad was a Christian. She had modeled her faith and taught him well. But his father was an alcoholic. I knew that soon

Brad's father would be his only parental guardian. That distressed me. It ripped out my heart.

"I am trusting that God will take care of my boy," she said. Her words were spoken softly, but also with conviction.

Amazing, I thought to myself. Our minds were tracking together, thinking of the same person. "Yes, God will take care of Brad," I repeated. My words came out fast. But pangs of fear raced through my heart. I doubted God. How could God take away the only stable person in Brad's life?

I know that we are not supposed to question God, but in my finite mind I could not comprehend how this could work out for good—for Brad's good. Brad's father was dysfunctional. In fact, at this critical moment in his wife's life, where was he? He wasn't even here at the hospital.

I held Pat's hand, stroking its backside with my other hand. I wanted to connect with her, to let her know how much I truly cared for and loved her. She smiled back. I stayed with Pat for another hour, passing the time quietly. Nobody came in to interrupt us—no nurses, doctors, technicians, or aides…nobody. It was special. I then gave her a hug and left.

The next day I learned that Pat had passed away sometime during the night. She was now with the Lord.

THE PROBLEM OF FAITH

Anyone who enters into the ministry of biblical hospitality will soon have his or her faith tested. The ministry is more demanding than anyone can imagine. The problems in people's lives seem, at times, to be overwhelming and unsolvable. Dark clouds form and seem to stretch to the horizon.

I faced this problem with the death of Pat. Now that she was dead, I could only see Brad being raised by an alcoholic father who would, I was convinced, shatter Brad's spirit and destroy his future. The little that Ken and I could do would be minute compared to the negative impact that Brad's father might have on him.

It is easy to read about faith in a book or hear it preached in a sermon. It is something else when you face problems and haven't a clue how they could be solved. It is here where faith is tested and where people have the opportunity to grow in faith.

Looking back, I now know that God was in control. Everyone's soul is a battleground—of many sorts. The point for each one of us is whether we will hang in there, as did Job, and say, "Though he slay me, yet will I trust in him."

Faith is a steadfast belief that behind each and every action stands God.

A great difference exists between our Christian experience and our Christian faith. If we rest our faith in our experiences, we will assuredly fall. But if we rest our faith in the great doctrines of God found in the Bible, we will remain standing.

We should never bargain with God—"I will do this, God, if you do that." God doesn't bargain.

We should be careful not to say, "Yes, but..." to God. We should always put a period on a sentence after saying yes. Our faith will be stretched. At times we will want to give up. But, Lord willing, we will continue onward—to the glory of God. He will see us through to the end.

After I learned that Pat was now with the Lord in heaven, I recalled a thought that crossed through my mind during my final visit with her. I heard the Spirit of God say to me: "I want you and Ken to raise Brad."

The words made me think of the story of Elijah and Elisha in the Old Testament, where Elijah's mantle was passed on to Elisha at the time when Elijah was summoned home to be with the Lord. I felt that Brad was being passed from Pat to Ken and me.

But were these words truly of the Lord? Sometimes I run ahead of God, and I have to be careful. After all, Ken and I already had five of our own children. And Brad was biracial. Would it work? I kept these questions to myself. Then, several months after the funeral, we received a call at two thirty in the morning. It was Brad.

"Would you come and pick me up?" he asked. "My dad and his girlfriend are having a big fight. I can't sleep."

"We'll be right over," I said. Twenty minutes later, we showed up in front of his house, and he met us at our car. He had his schoolbooks, clothes, and baseball uniform in hand.

This scene of Brad calling us in the middle of the night was repeated multiple times in the following weeks. We'd get a call, we'd show up at the house, and we'd take Brad to our home. Brad's father's world was alcohol.

Then I heard the Spirit of God speak to me a second time. He said: "I want you and Ken to raise Brad." This time, I said yes to the Lord. And, to my surprise, Ken also said yes—without reservation. The first chance that came my way, I asked Brad: "Would you like to live with us or stay with your father?" At first, he had no answer. I told him to think about it for a few days. But, a few hours later, he came to me and said, "Yes, I want to live with you, Mr. and Mrs. Loerop." Brad's father, as it turned out, was OK with this idea too. Brad then became the sixth child that I had prayed for even before we were married. God answers prayers in mysterious ways.

Chapter Three

SAYING YES TO THE LORD

Brad was a gift from the Lord. We were blessed by his presence. It is a world of *agape* (ah-GAH-pay) love.

What makes agape love special? Its primary characteristic is self-sacrifice. It is best seen at the cross of Jesus: "This is love: not that we loved God, but that he loved us and sent his Son as an atoning sacrifice for our sins" (1 John 4:10). Agape love has the peculiar ability to both broaden and break our hearts. Because it is a selfless love, it confronts those areas of selfishness deep within our souls. And, oddly, agape love is addictive. The more we experience it, the more we want it. This is because, with agape love, we begin to see the world the way God sees the world, with God-anointed eyes (1 John 4:8, 16).

But agape love also opens us up to new hurts. It can disappoint, disrupt, frustrate, break, and bruise. It is then, when our hearts break, that our faith is once again tested: "Is it worth it? Do I really need this?" we ask. The answer, of course, is "Yes." This is what agape love is all about—meeting the special needs of the people who God brings our way and doing for them what God has done for us.

But saying yes to the Lord is a battle that must be waged in each Christian's life on a daily basis. "Once you say yes to the Lord," writes Donna Otto, "you won't know exactly where you end up."[5] Kay Warren adds:

> *If denying yourself is all about saying no, then taking up the cross is all about saying yes: "Yes, God, I will do whatever you ask of me—whatever, whenever." It's agreeing with God that his way is best in every situation and choosing to obey him*

over every other authority, regardless of how you feel about it.[6]

This dying of self-will and opening to agape love (with all its blessings and hurts) does not come easily to any of us. Our sinful nature is so committed to its own well being that agape love seems foreign and nasty. It takes years of obedience in both the big and little things of life before agape love will begin to feel natural to many of us.

When we decided to become Brad's guardians, our decision did not include legal guardianship. It did not even include a formalized letter from Brad's father giving us permission to care for Brad. It was strictly an oral agreement.

One important detail involved the safeguarding of Brad's social security monies. Brad and I visited with a social worker in Oak Park to see if the money could be sent to his Uncle Doug in California. We hoped that he would serve as the financial trustee, keeping the money safe until Brad would need it for college tuition. To our amazement, Brad's father did not object. He was OK with Uncle Doug serving as trustee.

Ken and I treated Brad as a member of the family. It was not easy for Brad to come into a family of five children; neither was it exactly easy for us. Like many teens, communication could be a challenge. But professional counseling proved to be an effective tool to assist Brad.

During this time, it became apparent that Brad needed orthodontic work done. I drove him a number of times to the Loyola School of Dentistry. Along with my other children, he needed this dental care. At this time of my life, I was the taxi driver to sports, work, and dental appointments.

At Calvin College, Brad met his future wife, Sue. They now have five boys, including triplets. And they

Chapter Three

recently adopted identical twin girls. He graduated from Calvin with a business major. After a couple years of marriage, he came to believe that God was moving in his heart to be a math teacher rather than staying with his sales job at Steelcase. So Brad decided to go back to college. After receiving his teaching degree, Brad taught math and served as department chair at two different public high schools.

In June of 1989, Brad said good-bye to his Timothy Christian classmates. Little did he know that twenty-three years later, in the spring of 2012, the school board would offer Brad a contract to become the school principal at his alma mater. He enthusiastically said, "Yes." None of us in our family would have imagined that this thirteen-year-old boy would one day be the principal of our local Christian high school.

Brad has a heart for the homeless. Frequently, he makes peanut butter and jelly sandwiches and goes into Chicago to feed the homeless with his sons. One year, he took his family to Grand Rapids, Michigan, for a month of their summer vacation. During this time, they served in homeless shelters and food kitchens. In addition, he and his family faithfully attend a church in their community.

The story is not over yet. Our family went on a mission trip to the Dominican Republic from December 26, 2012, to January 1, 2013. Ken and I believed that this Christmas most of our grandchildren were of age to *give* rather than to *receive*, and we wanted to celebrate our fiftieth wedding anniversary by giving back to others. So we bought twenty-three tickets for our first family mission trip of three generations with most of the family. On December 31, while Brad was leading our devotions that night at nine thirty, he received a text from his wife saying that the birth mother of the twins that they were going to adopt was in surgery. We immediately prayed for her. Thirty minutes later, Brad informed us that Elizabeth Jane and Rebecca Grace were born. There was much rejoicing both in Illinois and in the Dominican Republic. God showed us again that his timing of the birth of these twins was the best. If they had arrived a few days earlier, Brad would have had to fly back to the United States earlier than planned to sign papers. The girls are healthy and well. God is so good all the time. Our missionary friends, the Van Tils, shared in our joy. A family of seven is now a family of nine.

> **MEDITATION**
> *"As I have loved you, so you must love one another. By this all men will know that you are my disciples, if you love one another"* (John 13:34–35).

QUESTIONS FOR PERSONAL REFLECTION OR GROUP DISCUSSION

1. In the eleventh chapter of Hebrews, Noah's faith was tested (v. 7). How was he tested? What would he have likely chosen to do if he had allowed human logic to guide his thinking?

2. In the eleventh chapter of Hebrews, Abraham's faith was repeatedly tested (vv. 8–19). How was he tested? What would he have likely chosen to do if he had allowed human logic to guide his thinking?

3. In the eleventh chapter of Hebrews, Moses's faith was repeatedly tested (vv. 24–29). How was he tested? What would he have likely chosen to do if he had allowed human logic to guide his thinking?

4. In what respect are those to whom we minister gifts from the Lord? How do these people typically stretch our faith and love?

5. What is it about agape love that is so attractive? Why is it the identifying mark of true Christianity? (John 13:34–35).

6. What steps of faith have you taken in your life? How have these steps impacted you years later?

7. Did you experience disappointment or blessings when you invested your time in the life a child?

Chapter Four

DON'T DO IT ALONE

On a warm Friday morning in the summer of 1987, I received a phone call. Mary, our church secretary, wanted me to know that a homeless couple and four children were walking along North Avenue. "They could be in danger," she added.

"Tell the family that I will meet them in the nearby park," I replied.

Immediately I packed an extra-large lunch with bananas, bread, and peanut butter and jelly, and loaded my station wagon with our three younger children. Off we went to meet this homeless family on Friday afternoon. As I drove down the road, I thought about my children. At the very least, I said to myself, my own children would see some homeless people up close and recognize how blessed we are to have a roof over our heads each night.

A few minutes later, we were at the park. Indeed, this family of six was homeless and starving. They quickly ate the food, and then the father explained to me that their last name was Beck and they had just come up from Montgomery, Alabama. Some people in a nearby apartment complex were their friends and had promised them a job. But the job did not materialize. Now they were on the streets.

I invited the Beck family to church on Sunday morning and told them that they were welcome to come over for dinner after the service. They were excited by the invitation, even though they did not know what to expect. I was a stranger to them, but the thought of food seemed to override any concerns about me.

I thought of a time when I was sixteen years old and was not permitted to invite a certain family to church because they were poorly dressed and had body odor. This was an opportunity to correct that past wrong.

On Sunday morning, I went to the park and picked up the Beck family at nine fifteen. They were anticipating my arrival. The night before, as they had previous nights, they slept in the park. I knew that they had no change of clothing and that the clothing that they were wearing was ragged and unkempt. I thought of Jesus's parable in which the master told his servants to go out in the streets and invite anyone to the wedding banquet. I trusted that my church would emulate Jesus's call to hospitality and receive this family with love.

The Becks sat with my family in one long pew. Elaine, the mother, seemed to enjoy the worship service. Her husband, Frank, didn't say much. And the children found sitting in a pew for one hour to be a real test of endurance. Alan, the oldest, found it the most difficult to sit still. Bubba, the youngest, went to the nursery. Sophie was quiet, but William had many questions and was a talker. I enjoyed introducing them

Chapter Four

to my friends, and they were well received as part of the family of God.

Following the worship service, we went home for supper. It is our custom to put a roast in the oven on Sunday mornings without knowing who might show up for dinner. God always put people in our path to invite, and today was no different. The Becks enjoyed a delicious, traditional Dutch dinner with roast beef, mashed potatoes, green string beans, and applesauce. Our kitchen table was indeed full with a dozen people. As we ate, I imagined that sitting at a table in a formal setting was not the norm for them.

That evening, Ken and I returned the family to the park. I had a difficult time sleeping. I was in a bed with a roof over my head, and the Beck family was sleeping in a park under the stars. The next several days I brought them food; but still, I was concerned for their personal hygiene and safety. Finally, I called one of our deacons and asked if there was something more that we as a church could do.

Dave B. said, "It has been some time since we have sponsored a family. Maybe we should take a serious look at this situation." He and the other deacons met together and began looking for an apartment for the Beck family.

Knowing that the full responsibility for the family was not on our shoulders and the deacons were now working with us in addressing this situation, Ken and I felt more comfortable. We invited the family into our home for a few days, which turned into weeks. Our basement became a "haven for the homeless." We placed a few mattresses on the floor and gave the children sleeping bags. We also provided a small table where they could have a few snacks. They ate all their meals upstairs with us in the kitchen. Our grocery bill doubled. But that was OK.

The next Sunday, a request was put in the church bulletin asking if someone could help find employment for Frank. One of our members who worked at Spiegel offered him a job. Yet, in order for that to happen, a job application had to be completed. Since Frank was illiterate, I helped him complete the application. Inquiring about his previous job, he said that he was a "chicken catcher." We both had a chuckle when he said that, and I wondered how that would qualify him to do anything at Spiegel. At the bottom of the form, he signed his name with an X.

The deacons found an apartment for the Beck family. And, ironically, it happened to be near the park where I originally found them. Families from church helped furnish the apartment and provided some clean clothes. Another member of our church acquired a yellow Volkswagen for them so that they would have transportation.

Within a couple of weeks, the family began to settle down into suburban life, which was very different from their rural life in Alabama. There were no goats or chickens running around them. Frank worked in one of the Spiegel stores not far from the church. Elaine was a stay-at-home mom. The children were enrolled in school.

One day, an electrician, Jack, came to fix the dryer in their apartment. He reached his hand in the vent and, to his surprise, out came the remains of a dead guinea pig. Elaine said that animals had the freedom to come and go in the rural homes of Alabama. She assumed the same was true here in the Chicago suburbs. Expecting them to adjust from life in Alabama to suburban Chicago in such a short time was quite a tall order.

Spiritual Gifts

Spiritual gifts are empowerments given by the Holy Spirit to all believers. Through these spiritual gifts, Christians effectively build up the body of Christ and extend the kingdom of God in this world. A list of the gifts is found in the Epistle to the Romans:

> *We have different gifts, according to the grace given us. If a man's gift is prophesying, let him use it in proportion to his faith. If it is serving, let him serve; if it is teaching, let him teach; if it is encouraging, let him encourage; if it is contributing to the needs of others, let him give generously; if it is leadership, let him govern diligently; if it showing mercy, let him do it cheerfully. (Romans 12:6–8)*

All of us, provided that we are true believers, have been blessed with at least one of these gifts.

Though knowing one's spiritual gift (or gifts) is useful information, we should not limit our work for God to only those areas of our giftedness. We should also serve the Lord wherever we are needed. In the early church, for example, Timothy was the pastor of the church in Ephesus, yet he did not have the gift of evangelism (preaching the Gospel). Still, the Apostle Paul admonished him: "Do the work of an evangelist" (2 Timothy 4:5).

If you don't have the gift of mercy, still show mercy. If you don't have the gift of giving, give what you can. If you don't have the gift of service, help out however possible. We should serve in the areas of our strengths, and, when needs arise, in the areas where we are weak. We serve, and the Holy Spirit gives us the ability to do what is required.

> People endowed with spiritual gifts enable a church to operate as a team, each gift complementing the others.

Heartfelt Hospitality

With this family from Alabama, a number of members of the church pitched in. The net result was a ministry effort in authentic hospitality that truly served a needy family.

Little by little, progress was made with the Beck family. Elaine brought the children to church faithfully each Sunday. Bubba attended Little Lambs, our midweek evangelistic ministry to preschoolers.

One Sunday evening, Ken went to pick up the Beck family for church. Yet, when Elaine and the children entered the car, Ken noticed a horrific odor. He immediately opened the window. Elaine then confessed that the cat had just urinated on Bubba. Ken drove home as quickly as possible, hoping to find me so I could help with this new emergency. But I had already left for church with our children. He then went upstairs and found some of my perfume and doused Bubba with half of the bottle. Finally, he arrived at church with the family. They found their spot in the pew where the children and I were already seated.

"What took you so long?" I whispered to him. "The cat peed on Bubba," he answered. This message was quickly passed down the pew, from each child to the next. Moments later, the entire pew began shaking, since nobody could keep the laughter to himself or herself. And since we were in the third pew from the front of the church, we became a spectacle, a disturbance to the entire worship service. I imagine that our pastor could not understand why the Loerop family was so disrespectful that particular Sunday evening in church.

Three years later, Elaine became pregnant and gave birth to a beautiful baby girl, Melissa. In the hospital, when I held her in my arms, I sang: "Jesus Loves Me." This is a tradition that I have done with each of my precious grandchildren. By singing that song, I said to myself that she had become my grandchild.

Then, four years after we met the Becks, a new problem arose. Due to the frequent absenteeism of the children from school, a social worker was sent over to assess the situation. She arrived at their apartment at ten o'clock in the morning. Elaine requested that she return at two that afternoon. By the time she returned, however, Frank and Elaine had put all five of the children in the Volkswagen and headed off to Alabama. They were in such a hurry that they left all of their clothes, furniture, photos, and earthly belongings behind due to the possible threat from the Department of Children and Family Services.

Two months later, I received a phone call from Elaine. Crying hysterically, she said, "Frank has just been murdered. Someone cut the brake line of the Volkswagen, and he hit a tree and was killed instantly." She was in such a mournful state that no words could comfort her. She had no money to even bury him. What a dramatic scene to live through. Christopher and Allen survived the car accident but had witnessed the death of their father. I assured Elaine I would support her through my prayers.

While we were in Florida in 2011 with our children, I called home and listened to my answering machine. It was Elaine Beck, and she asked that I return a phone call to her. We had had no contact for thirty years, so I thought that this must have been an important message. When I called her, she was crying uncontrollably and said, "William has been murdered." We cried together and prayed. Fortunately, in a couple of days, we would be leaving for Chicago, and I could meet her at a Wal-Mart near her hometown in Alabama.

I called her when Ken and I were getting close to the correct exit so that we could be there at approximately the same time. Seeing nobody that we recognized at Walmart, we walked over to the food court. Then I heard the familiar voice: "Jane." I turned around and saw tears streaming down Elaine's face. I met her second husband, to whom she had been married for the last seventeen years, and her daughter, Melissa, who was now in her early twenties.

Retelling the story was a way of grieving for Elaine. In the Wal-Mart food court, she relived the death of her son through many tears. We cried together. She wrote everything out for me as it had happened, step by step. He had been shot twice. Law enforcement never did a thorough investigation of the murder scene. "It was all so very crooked," Elaine said. "The individual who murdered my son drove my son around while he was still alive and then took him to his brothers. The police lied and just covered things up, and no one will ever know the truth."

As Elaine and I talked, she told Ken and me that the biggest mistake of her life was when they left Elmhurst and returned to Alabama. I thought, yes, I too wish that they had stayed.

I then asked her if she had any requests for Ken and me. She only asked us to send her the Bible on CD. Her current husband was also illiterate, yet he wanted to understand the Bible.

Months later, I received a phone call from Elaine. She said that they had received our gift of the Bible on CD. The Bible had made their faith come alive. They were now excited to understand the Bible stories, and attending church brought them joy. They are bringing the grandchildren to church with them. Sophie is attending church regularly with her children.

Success: What Is It?

I have often asked myself: was my church's involvement with this family from Alabama a success or a failure?

Indeed, the story had some strange twists and turns. And, after leaving Elmhurst and returning to Alabama, Frank and William were murdered.

I have concluded that when it comes to the question of success, Christian ministry is difficult to measure. The bottom line is found in neither numbers nor money; the important thing is obedience to the Lord and the degree to which the ministry brought glory and honor to God. How does one accurately measure this? "Try to excel in gifts that build up the church" (1 Corinthians 14:12).

- A number of people in the church, each with differing spiritual gifts, took part in helping Frank and Elaine.
- Many tangible resources were used, all of which were a testimony to the church's commitment to agape love.
- My children took an active role in ministering to this family and grew in their love for this family.
- I still frequently receive opportunities to encourage Elaine over the phone.

Our responsibility was to plant the seed. It was the Lord's responsibility to give the increase. And when we reflect back on this family, we can heartily give thanks unto the Lord for the opportunity to serve in his name.

> **MEDITATION**
> Try to excel in gifts that build up the church.

Questions for Personal Reflection or Group Discussion

1. List each of the spiritual gifts found in Romans 12:6–8. In what ways can each of these gifts benefit the ministry of radical hospitality?

2. Should Christians involve themselves in the ministry of biblical hospitality if they do not feel they are being called to use their gifts in this manner?

3. In your opinion, was the church's ministry in the lives of Frank, Elaine, and their children a success or a failure? Why?

4. Was it too much to expect a family from rural southern culture to adjust to suburban culture in Chicago? What could have been done to make this transition easier for them?

5. Was there a point in the story where you would have walked away and given up?

6. When tragedy strikes, what is the best way to empathize with individuals?

Chapter Five

FACING FAILURE

*E*arly one day, at about five in the morning, Ken opened the garage door, and he prepared to leave for work in downtown Chicago. Blocking the driveway, however, was a car with a small trailer. In the trailer were all the earthly goods of a former prison convict who had been with us during a release program with Prison Fellowship six months earlier. In the car were Stan (the former convict), his wife, Marge, and their five children.* They needed a place to stay.

Though we agreed to make contact with Stan after his release from prison, we did not have any plan of commitment between him and us or what it would involve. Ken invited them inside. After a lengthy conversation, we said yes, they could stay with us.

Prison Fellowship had assured us that the only paroled prisoners who participated in this reentry into society were born-again Christians. They had only committed white-collar crimes. But questions entered our minds. Should we leave the knives in the drawers? Should we hide our credit cards? And what about the children? At that time, we had one teenage girl, an elementary-age girl, and three boys. As we struggled with these thoughts, our son, K. J., offered us some degree of comfort. "Sure, Mom," he said. "This would be really cool. Let's do it!" K. J. was always open for an adventure.

While Stan was in prison, Marge had moved to Kansas to be closer to her husband. Yet she did not have any money. She rented an apartment for two hundred dollars a month and got a job at a bakery. This job, however, didn't last long, since the manager treated her poorly and she had been making more money on welfare. So she quit.

But when the owner of the bakery learned how she had been treated while on the job, he fired the manager and hired her back as manager with double the salary. However, when her husband was released from prison, she moved to Illinois hoping to start life over. Both of them were now seeking employment.

We made sure that Stan, Marge, and the children felt welcome in our home. Stan had a winning personality, and he especially won the heart of our youngest son, Mark, who was seven years old. Marge was a gifted musician and often sang religious melodies that she had written.

Still, I was cautious with Stan. I could not get his criminal background out of my mind. I think part of my problem was the way he responded to people. He was a smooth talker, always looking for a clever angle, always needing to be right, and never really showing humility. I arranged my daily schedule so that I was never alone with him in the house.

Our church assisted us with the care of this family. The deacons made arrangements for the children to attend a private Christian school. Each morning, Marge and I lined up ten brown paper bags for the children to take their lunches to school. Filling ten bags with sandwiches, snacks, and fruit each day was no small task. Even though we had three washrooms, they did not seem sufficient to get everyone properly groomed before heading off to school.

Part of our routine was to gather in the family room once a day for circle prayer time. We held hands, joined hearts, and prayed earnestly for the needs that lay ahead of us each day. It was our way of committing one another to the will of God and asking God's blessing in each one's life.

Taking Risks

Serious ministry always involves some degree of risk. Just ask a Christian worker serving God in an inner city mission or a missionary working in a foreign country. They are in those difficult places, they say, because God has called them. To be sure, they minimize the risk as much as possible. But risk never goes away… completely.

It is no different with the ministry of biblical hospitality. At times, we open our homes to people like Stan. They are repentant, or so they say, but we are never quite sure. They say all the right things, but their actions speak otherwise. We are always left double-checking our credit cards, cash, and other valuables—making sure that they are where they are supposed to be.

We worked on our daily schedules, making sure that people were not left alone with Stan, where temptation could overcome him and something horrible could happen.

Still, this is part and parcel with this kind of ministry. We need to understand this, and the sooner the better. I am thankful that in the forty years that my family and I have been engaged in the ministry of radical hospitality that none of us has ever been assaulted and none of our possessions have been stolen. But that does not mean that it could not have happened, or that it might not yet happen sometime in the future.

One Christian put it this way: "Being a Christian is often a risk in itself, but actively sharing God's Word, even though it is what God has commanded, adds personal risk…Every time believers reach out in the name of Christ, we are accepting the risk that is involved, whether at home or on the other side of the world."[7]

Jesus said: "Go! I am sending you out like lambs among wolves" (Luke 10:3).

Love is bold.

Stan joined our family activities and went to Bible studies and events arranged by Prison Fellowship. But it soon became apparent that this family needed an apartment of their own. They found one, and off they went to their new residence.

In the case of Stan, he had a demanding personality and treated his wife horribly. I remember spending hours with Marge, and repeatedly she told me that she could never see herself leaving Stan. However, she also said that she could not continue living under the verbal abuse that she was experiencing on a daily basis.

Then a new host of problems emerged. Stan told Marge that he wasn't going to support the family anymore. He made no effort whatsoever to pay any of the bills. The straw that broke the camel's back was when Stan provoked one of his sons to hit him. The son went into the shower to get away from him only to find his father in the bathroom waiting for him to emerge from the shower stall. When he emerged, the conflict reignited. The son hit his father in the head and ran. When Stan threatened to have his own son arrested, Marge said to herself: "That's enough!" She filed for divorce.

Following the divorce, she joined Women Against Domestic Abuse and helped form a chapter called Citizens Against Domestic Abuse. She was later voted in as an aide to a state representative in Wisconsin to fight against domestic abuse.

THE "WHAT IF" SYNDROME

When marriages of people under our care crumble, it is almost a reflex action for us to look at ourselves and wonder whether we were a part of the problem. What did we say? What did we do? What if we had said this instead of that? What if we had given them just a little more of our time? What if we had admonished them just a little stronger? What if…what if…what if…

The hardest part in serving God with heartfelt hospitality is the deep emotional lows that we enter into when those who we love and serve enter into deep disobedience to God. What is more, on occasion, they not only turn against God, but they also turn against us. We become the punching bag.

When this happens, what are we to do? Once again, Jesus is our example. Listen to the Apostle Peter:

> *But if you suffer for doing good and you endure it, this is commendable before God. To this you were called, because Christ suffered for you, leaving you an example, that you should follow in his steps…When they hurled their insults at him, he did not retaliate; when he suffered, he made no threats. Instead, he entrusted himself to him who judges justly. (1 Pet. 2:20, 21, 23)*

It's healthy that we ask such questions. Maybe we did say or do something that was not appropriate. After all, we are certainly not sinless. And consider the alternative: a calloused inner spirit that is never willing to look at faults in ourselves. And when Stan and Marge's marriage broke apart and ended in divorce, my heart also broke.

I have learned that in these situations it is best to emotionally let go of the family or individual and move on. People come to us with myriads of problems, many of them rooted deeply in their past. We can love them, provide for their immediate needs, share the Gospel with them, and encourage them to go on with God. Yet we cannot bring them to repentance.

In other words, let God sort it out. He may send people our way who will show us our failings. Other times, we may experience successes. Whatever the case, we will stand before the Lord in the afterlife, and he will speak to us. And when he speaks, I am sure that he will comment on our desires to be used by him in the lives of other people. These words, I am sure, will be quite comforting to us.

So in the meantime, we are to follow the example of Jesus. We are not to retaliate, and we are not to make threats. This is the way in which we are to handle ourselves.

Just prior to his arrest and crucifixion, Jesus spoke some important words to his disciples. He said: "In this world you will have trouble. But take heart! I have overcome the world" (John 16:33). When we face such troubles, we are commanded to take heart. What does that mean? Taking heart, I believe, means many things:

- to think hopefully;
- to strengthen our resolve;
- to continue the fight;
- to never call retreat;
- to not give up, no matter what; and
- to never stop loving.

We who are involved in heartfelt hospitality must be people who know what it means to "take heart." We need to memorize those two words from the Gospel of John and meditate upon them often.

I am sure that Jesus followed his own advice and *took heart* the night that Judas Iscariot betrayed him with a kiss (Luke 22:48). And I am sure that the Apostle Paul *took heart* when he learned that one of his trusted coworkers, Demas, had deserted him because he loved this world more than the things of God (2 Timothy 4:10).

The conclusion to the story has a bright side. Marge did remarry a fine Christian man, and they are writing Christian songs together. To the best of my knowledge, at least two of their five children are dedicated Christians. So we do take heart.

Meditation

Each and every ministry has its moments when people are called up to face extraordinary challenges and take an extraordinary amount of courage. Jesus calls this *taking heart*. It is the opposite of losing heart or melting in fear.

"For everyone born of God overcomes the world" (1 John 5:4).

QUESTIONS FOR PERSONAL REFLECTION OR GROUP DISCUSSION

1. In your own words, explain what *taking heart* means to you.

2. What precautions can you take to minimize risk when inviting someone into your home for an extended period of time?

3. According to the New Testament, does God expect Christians to engage in some degree of risk when exercising their faith?

4. When people under our care fail to follow the Lord, what is an appropriate course of action?

5. Reporting and reacting to abuse are very painful and sensitive issues in anyone's life. But it must be acknowledged and dealt with rather than denied. Have you or a friend ever dealt with an abusive situation? How did you protect the innocent person?

*All the names in this chapter have been changed.

Chapter Six

JOE FROM SKID ROW

When I think of the term *skid row*, images emerge in my mind of the rough parts of a town, a place full of bars and accented with brothels, garbage, bottles of liquor that are emptied and scattered everywhere, and broken lives. Those who frequently live in its streets are typically homeless, and their day-to-day existence is rummaging through garbage and hoping that someone passing by will give them a little money.

Joe* lived in such an area. He said that he was an "evil person" and his life was in frequent danger. Bullets flew past his head more than once. In order to survive on skid row, he would go through garbage cans to look for food. If he saw a man with a narrow brown bag, he knew that this person was carrying a bottle of whisky, gin, wine, or some such thing. He would knock the man down, grab the bottle, and drink it himself to drown his troubles.

Then one day, Joe decided to go to the Helping Hand Mission in Chicago. While at the mission, a fellow by the name of Clarence led him to the Lord. Joe memorized and claimed Jeremiah 29:11 as his life verse. The verse says: "For I know the plans I have for you, declares the Lord, plans to prosper you and not to harm you, plans to give you hope and a future."

However, Joe still struggled with anger. One day, he gruffly said to God in prayer: "Where are those wonderful plans, God?"

Soon afterward, he picked up the *Banner*, a church magazine, and read an advertisement for a church custodian. He called the number in the ad and asked for the job. To his surprise, Elmhurst Christian Reformed Church (my church!) had put that ad in the magazine. The church leadership agreed to interview Joe. Several elders drove down to the Helping Hand Mission and spoke with him. Then, after prayerful consideration, the elders agreed to hire him.

My husband, Ken, was an elder at the church at the time, and he was given the job of driving down to the rescue mission to pick up Joe. On a grim, dark night, Ken drove into Chicago to find the mission. Because of good directions, he found it without too much effort.

Joe was unshaven and wore tattered clothes, and he was Hispanic. On the way back to Elmhurst, Joe praised God, thrilled over the opportunity to get an honest job. Ken heard him say repeatedly, "Amen, Brother!" when asked questions. He left his homeless environment and came to us with only the clothes that he wore, plus a few items tied in a knot like a duffel bag. This was the total of his earthly belongings.

Chapter Six

I was thrilled. What a great way to begin mixing the nationalities of our church, which at that time was primarily Dutch in membership. Our pastor at the time, Wayne Leys, also welcomed Joe.

Once Joe arrived at church, he needed a place to eat and sleep. We emptied the vacation Bible school closet behind the balcony and put a fold-up cot in it to serve as his bedroom. Members of the church bought food for him and placed it in a refrigerator in the kitchen.

I gave Joe haircuts and helped him when he was ill. Almost every Sunday, he had dinner with us. When we forgot he was coming, we scraped some of the food off of the children's plates, opened the door, and welcomed him in. He always had a full plate of food. He never knew that it was leftover food from our children's plates.

Now a Christian, Joe thought about a child he had fathered from a previous marriage and his delinquency in making child support payments. He hardly ever saw his child. Indeed, the challenges before him seemed mountainous. How would God ever turn Joe's life around?

For Joe, having a place to work, eat, and sleep was nothing but an answer to prayer. Since I worked at the church several days during the week, our family left many meals in the refrigerator for him. All the necessities of life were now available to our new custodian from skid row. He was a blessing to us, and we were a blessing to him. He became like part of our family.

Joe tried his best. But his best was not as good as his new employer expected. I often checked his work and either dusted the areas that he missed or pointed those areas out to him. I wanted him to experience success, as well as show him how to do his job in a way that would please the church council. He did achieve and accomplish this goal.

But often Joe would say, "I feel so lonely, Jane. Please pray that God would someday give me a godly wife." He got his life in order and paid his debts. Then God honored his prayer request. One day he was sitting in McDonald's and met a woman who would become his wife.

The Least of These

As I mentioned earlier in this book, heartfelt hospitality has nothing in common with the notion of hospitality described by Emily Post or Martha Stewart. Rather, we should think of it as a spiritual hospital, where those who have been broken down or crushed by the hard knocks of life are shown the way back to God.

The Gospel of Jesus Christ is good news indeed.

We show people the way to heaven, as well as God's love in this life. And this includes those who are the poorest of the poor, those who occupy the bottom of our society. Scripture makes this point forcefully.

Solomon: "He who oppresses the poor shows contempt for their Maker, but whoever is kind to the needy honors God" (Prov. 14:31).

Moses: "When you have finished setting aside a tenth of all your produce in the third year, the year of the tithe, you shall give it to the Levite, the alien, the fatherless and the widow, so that they may eat in your towns and be satisfied" (Deut. 26:12).

Jesus: "When you give a banquet, invite the poor, the crippled, the lame, the blind, and you will be blessed. Although they cannot repay you, you will be repaid at the resurrection of the righteous" (Luke 14:13, 14).

Job: "If I have denied the desires of the poor or let the eyes of the widow grow weary, if I have kept my bread to myself, not sharing it with the fatherless—but from my youth I reared him as would a father, and from my birth I guided the widow—if I have seen anyone perishing for lack of clothing, or a needy man without a garment, and his heart did not bless me for warming him with the fleece from my sheep, if I have raised my hand against the fatherless, knowing that I had influence in court, then let my arm fall from the shoulder, let it be broken off at the joint" (Job 31:16–22).

And this, of course, is why so many rescue missions, soup kitchens, and the like exist in many inner cities. Churches support these ministries with their monies and human resources precisely because Christ died for the entire world, including those who live on skid row.

But we are missing out if all we do is help keep the rescue missions operative. Sooner or later, the poor and needy in rescue missions need to be re-assimilated into our churches and communities. This is another side to heartfelt hospitality. In our case, the possibility of Joe becoming part of our church family fell into our laps. We didn't seek him out; he sought us out. But at least we had the spiritual awareness to see the opportunity when it came.

As Joe grew in his relationship with Jesus Christ, he began to take part in the ministries of the church. One of the first things he did was go on a brief mission trip to Yucatan, Mexico. Since Joe was born in Mexico, he not only spoke Spanish fluently, he understood the Mexican culture and possessed a passion to minister to the Mexican people.

After his trip to Mexico, our friend Clair Van Zeelt asked him to consider getting involved in Prison Fellowship. Joe said, "Yes," and has been involved in this ministry for the past twenty-three years. He spent his time in Cell Blocks 3, 6, and 7 at the Cook County

Jail. This is where the inmates who speak Spanish as a first language are held. When he wasn't visiting the jail, he wrote letters to the inmates and corrected their Bible lessons.

In recent years, Joe and his new wife moved to a community some distance from Elmhurst. They now attend a church in their community where they live. And Joe has become an elder in that church.

We saw a sovereign God orchestrate the life of a very angry person with so much spiritual baggage to become a meek and mild husband, father, and grandfather. This happened through the work of the Spirit of God in Joe's life, who arranged many people to reach out and minister to him. Opening our home to Joe and seeing him transform before our eyes was nothing but a miracle to us and to our entire church.

MEDITATION

Our ministries must not neglect the poorest of the poor in our midst. Those who fail to minister to their needs miss the richest blessing. They might be living in disobedience to Christ.

QUESTIONS FOR PERSONAL REFLECTION OR GROUP DISCUSSION

1. What made it difficult for Joe to adjust to a church setting?

2. How would you have enfolded Joe into the life of your church?

3. What changes would you have required up front from Joe?

4. What type of follow-up would you have done in his life?

5. What would you have done to encourage him to take the next step to become more like Christ?

6. Do you have a friend who you can identify as being a "Joe"?

*All the names in this chapter have been changed.

Chapter Seven

DEALING WITH SELF-DESTRUCTION

Part of my Healing Hearts Ministry is to respond to pleas for food assistance. These calls always excite me because I consider them another avenue to share the Gospel, as well as meet a humanitarian need.

One day our church secretary received a call from the Willow Creek Community Church in Barrington. The message was transferred to the Healing Heart Ministry, on my answering machine. According to our church secretary, Mary, there was a woman who was in desperate need of food, and she lived only a few miles away from our church. I gathered food from our freezer and canned goods from my cupboard to take to her apartment. Without too much effort, I found her dwelling on the second floor of an apartment building. Our two youngest children went with me on another calling from the Lord.

Maria* met me at the door of her apartment, a huge smile on her face. To my astonishment, it looked like she weighed 350 pounds. Behind her were four thin, young children. Although I knew I was being judgmental, I couldn't help but think that Maria did not need the food—but her children did. I placed the food on her kitchen counter and then visited with her for a short time.

As we talked, I imagined that two of her youngest children might enjoy our evangelistic preschool ministry at my church called Little Lambs. And, the very youngest child, Marilyn, might enjoy our nursery while the others were in class. Since it was near the end of August, this would be a perfect time to enroll them. I assured Maria that this would be our love gift to them, and there would be no charge. She was quite happy to see them get some religious education, and I encouraged her to join Coffee Break, an interfaith Bible study for women that takes place at the same time as Little Lambs.

To my pleasant surprise, Maria was eager to meet other women and join this program. Before long, she made a profession of faith in Christ and joined our church. We had coffee at our home to celebrate this big event. She was noticeably pleased, since her husband and all of the children were present.

The requests for food continued to come, and we did meet the requests, trusting that she would share the food with her children. She claimed that her husband, José, did not make enough money to cover the rent, car expenses, and food.

One evening, José stopped by our house and shared his concern about the size of his wife and her inability to clean the house due to her weight. He said, "She has such a craving for food that it is like an obsession with her." He added that many times he found her going through the garbage alongside the apartment complex looking for more food, remnants that other people had thrown out. This craving was far beyond normal. He then asked if I had any suggestions.

I said that I would encourage her to begin an exercise regimen. I took her to a nearby park with her children, and we walked and walked. I hoped that this would also improve her mental attitude. And it did, to a point. I advised her to surrender her craving for food to the Lord and seek spiritual food in its place.

Because Maria was becoming less and less responsible toward her four children, she was assigned a social worker. For the sake of the children, a person was assigned to come to the apartment once a week to assist her with housecleaning.

But all the while, José was becoming desperate. He worked as a custodian at a local public school. He found it increasingly difficult to manage the family and his job. Finally, after much frustration, he had Maria committed to a mental health clinic at DuPage County Hospital.

During this time, Maria and José's boys stayed with Ken and me, and José's relatives cared for their two girls. Our goal was to love and guide the two sons, Johnny and Jimmy. Johnny slept in the same room as our son Mark and our dog, Charles. Jimmy slept in his own room.

Three weeks later, after Maria's release from the hospital, we were hopeful that things would improve— and they did for a while. Maria was an intelligent woman, but she was a compulsive eater. Her weight continued to increase. Unable to control his anger, José finally filed for divorce. Yet, even then, he begged me: "Can't something be done to change her?"

After the divorce, Maria moved to a reasonably priced apartment. Then, after two years, she was evicted because she could not pay the rent or keep the place free from rodents and roaches.

Since she was a friend of mine, I shared this new need with our church staff and asked them for their assistance in moving her.

My son, KJ, who was now a co-owner of a construction recycling business, provided a container free of charge to dispose of the garbage that had accumulated in her apartment. The church staff, under the leadership of Pastor Bert De Jong, worked as "servants of Christ" as they cleaned and threw the many unnecessary items into the dumpster. With little effort, they had no trouble filling the container to the brim.

In the meantime, Maria's mother passed away. She inherited some money and was able to rent a home in another neighboring community. By this time, Johnny was a junior in high school, and Jimmy was a freshman. The boys were getting involved in gangs and not attending school regularly. This added to José rage, who was already upset with Maria.

Everything came to a boiling point when José discovered that Maria, now his ex-wife, was pregnant by a male prostitute.

Weeks later, José visited Maria, said that his car would not start, and asked if he could stay overnight and sleep on the couch. While the children were sleeping, just after five in the morning, he killed Jimmy with a .22-caliber handgun. His two daughters were shot and left in critical condition. One of them survived. He then fired at his ex-wife and missed. With only one bullet left in his gun, he shot and killed himself. Since

Johnny, the oldest son, was not home that evening, he missed the terrible murder scene.

According to the authorities, José had no criminal record and appeared to be the most stable person in the family. This murder-suicide was a shock to the entire community.

Could things get worse? Johnny was found two days later hanging by his neck from a rope in a tree. He also had committed suicide. He was only sixteen years old.

Events like this rattle one's faith to its core. It causes one to question and rethink everything.

Where was God in all of this? Why didn't God intervene and stop the killings before they started? Did the church do enough? Did I do enough? Was Maria a genuine believer in Christ? What does it mean when God says in the Bible that he loves us with an everlasting love?

Many people who have experienced similar tragedies in life have responded by turning away from the Christian faith, believing it to be nothing more than a sham. Of all the children, Jimmy was the one to whom our family had drawn the closest, so it was especially painful when we heard that he had been killed. We thought that he had the most potential. Yet they were all valued by our family and loved by God equally.

Though I had many questions about God and the Christian faith after this experience, I did not doubt God's existence, his love, or the truth of the Gospel. Why? I had been prepared for events like this by years of good, sound biblical teaching. It helped me get through this time of deep darkness.

This side of heaven, we will never understand that God's ways are not our ways, yet God entered our lives through Jesus, who cared for people who were suffering. God does not always take away pain but shares it with us. This is a mystery known only to God himself. God has an eternal perspective that we cannot understand in our limited human minds.

Christians are not perfect, just forgiven.

Never confuse heaven with earth. Heaven is the place of rest. The earth is a place of spiritual warfare, tribulation, and persecution.

Never blame God for the hypocrisy and sinfulness of certain Christians, or the free will and choices of any person.

Not all people who claim to be Christians are the genuine article. If a transformation toward holiness does not begin to show following one's profession of faith, this should bring us to our knees and to commit them to prayer.

I firmly believe that anyone who takes biblical hospitality seriously will experience times of deep darkness and will have his or her faith rattled by that darkness. As we reach into the lives of sinful people, it is only a matter of time before their sinfulness impacts our lives as well.

More than anything else, we must remember that Jesus Christ is our example. In an epistle written to Christians suffering a season of serious persecution, the letter to the Hebrews stated:

> *Let us fix our eyes on Jesus, the author and perfecter of our faith, who for the joy set before him endured the cross, scorning its shame, and sat down at the right hand of the throne of God. Consider him who endured such opposition from sinful men, so that you will not grow weary and lose heart…Endure hardship as discipline; God is treating you as his children, for what children are not disciplined by their father?" (Hebrews 12:7)*

"Give ear to my words, O Lord, consider my sighing. Listen to my cry for help, my King and my God. In the morning, O Lord, you hear my voice; In the morning I lay my requests before you and wait in expectation" (Psalms 5:1–3).

> **MEDITATION**
> Whoever takes biblical hospitality seriously must care for his or her soul, being equipped with sound doctrine and much Scripture, in order to withstand the evil day when it comes.

QUESTIONS FOR PERSONAL REFLECTION OR GROUP DISCUSSION

1. The lives of the students of the high school where Johnny and Jimmy attended were never the same following the murder and suicides. How might God use this event in a positive way in their lives?

2. What suggestions would you give to Maria concerning her addiction to food?

3. Are you struggling with any addictions? If so, how are you seeking help?

4. What suggestions would you have given to José concerning his problems with his family?

5. Do we as a church take the time needed to truly minister to families who join our church? Or do we assume that once they are members, all is well? How can more personal attention be given to each individual person when a church accepts members?

6. Could marital counseling have prevented such a tragic ending?

*All the names in this chapter have been changed, except for our family, the pastor, and our son, K.J.

Chapter Eight

DIVINE INTERRUPTIONS

Wilson first met Tutuvi when he was vacationing in Ghana.* They quickly fell in love and were married. Perhaps they had gotten married too soon. At least, that is what their parents said. But they were young, in love, and did what they desired. Wilson then returned to the United States and said that he would arrange for Tutuvi's immigration papers so that she could join him.

Then Tutuvi discovered that she was pregnant. During childbirth, the baby died. Full of despair, she longed to be with Wilson. Yet the immigration process was slow and cumbersome. They talked on the phone, but the calls were far too brief. Then Wilson stopped calling and stopped receiving her calls. She wrote him letters, but he failed to write back. What was going on? She began to wonder whether or not he wanted to be married to her anymore. Tutuvi's mother kept her spirits alive by supporting her and helping her.

Finally, after two and a half years, Tutuvi's immigration to the United States was granted in 1995. Wilson returned to Ghana, and together they boarded a flight for Chicago. During the flight, he told her that in Chicago some other woman would be calling on the phone. This woman would claim to be his wife, he explained. But Tutuvi had no reason to worry—the caller was merely his first wife, and they were now divorced.

"What?" Tutuvi exclaimed. "Why didn't you tell me this before? If you are now divorced, why would she be calling, still claiming to be your wife?" Wilson had no answers. As she looked out the small airplane window and stared at the ocean below, she struggled to make sense of it all. Once they arrived in Chicago, she planned to purchase a ticket, board another flight, and return to Africa.

But when they arrived in Chicago, she changed her mind. They went straight to the apartment. "Everything will turn out OK," Wilson assured her.

The next day, while Wilson was at work, a woman named Helen called. "Hello," Tutuvi politely said. "Who is this?" the other woman demanded. "My name is Tutuvi. I'm Wilson's wife. Who are you?"

"My name is Helen," the woman replied and then abruptly hung up. The next day, she called again, and this time Wilson answered the phone. Their conversation was long and heated. Then, in a third phone call, Helen spoke with Tutuvi. As they spoke, Helen threatened to kill Tutuvi.

Once again, Tutuvi's world was turned upside down. Not only did she have serious questions about her marriage to Wilson, but she now feared for her life. Not knowing where to turn, she got a job at one of the local supermarkets—without Wilson's knowledge.

Chapter Eight

A worker in the store, Mary Lee, took a special liking to Tutuvi. Knowing that Tutuvi was deeply burdened, she asked her what was going on. At first, Tutuvi said nothing. Then, a few weeks later, she unburdened her soul and shared everything. The answer to her problems, Mary Lee explained, was for Tutuvi to become pregnant.

Tutuvi said, "No—a baby would just further complicate things." Eventually, though, she did become pregnant. And when Wilson learned of the pregnancy, he was not pleased. He showed no interest in her pregnancy and refused to take her to doctor appointments.

Then, in a fit of rage, he tore up all the wedding pictures. "Our relationship is worth nothing in my eyes," he told her.

Shortly after this, another woman from Ghana moved into the apartment. Wilson was now living in open adultery—with Tutuvi still in the home. When Tutuvi complained, Wilson shouted back and pushed her around. Again fearing for her life, Tutuvi called the police.

Upon their arrival, the police advised her to leave the apartment for her own safety. They asked if she had any good friends to help her. She remembered that she had a card in her purse that she had picked up when she was at the Elmhurst Christian Reformed Church. She gave the card to the police, and one of them called The Healing Hearts number.

I received the phone call from the police at about ten o'clock in the morning. I told the policeman that I would be at the apartment as soon as possible. When I arrived, I met the police and Tutuvi. I took Tutuvi to my home and put her to bed because she was badly stressed. I assured her she would be safe.

The next day, Ken and I took Tutuvi to the hospital to see an obstetrician since she was eight months pregnant. Due to the stress she had been under, the baby's heartbeat proved to be abnormal. She came back the following day the baby's heartbeat continued to be abnormal. Things were serious. The doctor explained that if Tutuvi did not have any contractions within the next day, he would have to deliver the baby in order to save Tutuvi's life

That night, I called for a special prayer meeting at church. Tutuvi stayed home with Ken and rested. While we were praying at church, her water broke. Ken drove her to the hospital, and I met her there. Together we joined hands and prayed, asking God that the blood pressure would drop and a healthy baby would be delivered.

Within an hour, a baby boy was delivered. Both mother and child were in good health. There was much rejoicing in that delivery room. I held little curly haired Dela in my arms and sang "Jesus Loves Me" to another precious child.

Tutuvi and Dela stayed with us for the next few months until I left for my trip to the Ukraine (see chapter twelve). She then flew back to Ghana, where Tutuvi's parents would raise Dela. Tutuvi returned to Chicago and finalized her divorce from Wilson.

Tutuvi got a job at a hospital in the United States as a certified nursing assistant and acquired a degree as a respiratory therapist. With her salary, she supported both her parents and Dela back in Ghana. Tutuvi was a born-again Christian, and we have been in contact with each other for many years. I receive e-mails and phone calls from her. To Tutuvi, I am her second mother and the grandmother of Dela.

Fifteen years later, Dela returned to the United States and was reunited with his mother. He is now doing very well in a private school and has mastered the English language. He feels deep gratitude for his mother, who persevered and his adopted American "grandparents."

When Dela turned sixteen, we included him in our family vacation. We brought him to our condo in Michigan, where he had his first experience with water toys—jet skiing, tubing, and boating. To our surprise, he managed to save our jet ski from floating away in the lake. He was a hero in our eyes in many ways.

DIVINE INTERRUPTIONS

I have learned that some of the most memorable moments in Scripture occurred as the result of divinely arranged interruptions. Consider the following:

> *While tending to their sheep in the fields near Bethlehem, an angel of the Lord suddenly appeared to a number of shepherds and announced to them that the Savior had been born, Christ the Lord. The angel also said that the baby could be found wrapped in cloths lying in a manger. The shepherds immediately left the sheep and sought out the baby. (Luke 2:8–15)*

> *Unexpectedly, Jesus and his twelve disciples arrived at the home of Lazarus, Martha, and Mary, in the town of Bethany. Caring for their needs was a major undertaking, considering their number. Yet, they did so. Martha was so overwhelmed by the work involved that she began to complain that Mary was not doing her fair share, which resulted in a rebuke to Martha from Jesus. (Luke 10:38–42)*

> *While traveling through Jericho with a large crowd, a blind man began to cry out, "Jesus, Son of David, have mercy on me!" Many people rebuked him and*

told him to be quiet, since Jesus was busy with other things. But the man cried out all the louder. Hearing the man, Jesus interrupted his business, spoke with him, and healed him of his blindness. (Mark 10:46–52)

While carrying the cross to Mount Calvary, Jesus collapsed to the ground. He could not continue any further. At that moment, a Roman soldier saw an able-bodied man, Simon, nearby and demanded that he help Jesus carry the cross. (Matt. 27:32)

What do we see in these four passages of Scripture?

On one occasion, the interruption required a number of men to set aside their professional work to do the will of God. On another occasion, the interruption resulted in grumbling and complaining on the part of one of Jesus's most beloved disciples. On a third occasion, the people surrounding Jesus sought to keep him from the interruption, believing that he had more important work to do. And in the final occasion, a man was forced to do that which he loathed: help carry the cross of a condemned man.

Dietrich Bonhoeffer writes:

We must be ready to allow ourselves to be interrupted by God. It is a strange fact that Christians and even ministers frequently consider their work so important and urgent that they allow nothing to disturb them. They think they are doing God a service in this, but actually they are disclaiming God's crooked yet straight path.[8]

Making ourselves available for divine interruptions begins with the mind and the heart. We need to be predisposed to allow God to interrupt our schedules and our routines.

This does not mean that we stop and help each and every person, but neither does it mean that we are so focused on our own plans that we never stop. We pray for the gift of discernment to be led by the Holy Spirit and then to act accordingly.

Making ourselves available for divine interruptions then carries forward into practical activities. We need to step out in faith and show ourselves to be available to the Lord. The Bible says, "I being in the way, the LORD led me" (Genesis 24:27, KJV).

In my case, I thought about the needy people in my community. Their needs are great: people with unplanned pregnancies, people in need of employment, people in need of childcare, people in need of food, people living in abusive homes, people living on the streets, people addicted to drugs or alcohol—the list goes on and on.

In 1991 my friend Linda and I established the Healing Heart Ministry. We have received hundreds of phone calls over the years. Each one, you might say, was an interruption to our schedules. But we see each interruption as an opportunity to be the hands and feet of Jesus to someone in need. On some occasions, as with Tutuvi, my husband and I went the extra mile and invited the people we helped to our home. For the past seventeen years, Tutuvi and Dela have been part of our extended family.

Our Use of Time

Time is a curious concept. One culture looks upon it one way, and another culture looks upon it in another way. I've been told that a lot of this has to do with the clock. Since its invention in the thirteenth century, the clock has changed the way people think about and organize their days. Everything now revolves around tight schedules. In America, almost everyone wears a wristwatch.

In the biblical world, however, people had no clocks. They studied the location of the sun and the moon in their arcs over the horizon to get an idea of time. Accordingly, schedules were not quite as tight. Punctuality was an almost unheard of concept.

So when the Apostle Paul tells us that we are to be "redeeming the time, because the days are evil" (Ephesians 5:16, KJV), he did not mean that we should maximize our use of each and every minute of the day. What he meant was that:

> We should maximize the opportunities to serve God that come our way each day.

I believe that the word translated as *time* would better be understood to mean "opportunities."

Sometimes our tight schedules get in the way of the opportunities that God brings our way to serve him. When our days are over, we look back in exhaustion and wonder what we actually accomplished that made any difference.

We, of course, cannot get rid of our clocks. But maybe we can strive to loosen up our schedules (at least a little) and watch for unexpected opportunities to serve God.

> **MEDITATION**
> Heartfelt hospitality is the willingness to redeem opportunities that come your way. These divine interruptions sometimes open doors to new ministries.

Chapter Eight

QUESTIONS FOR PERSONAL REFLECTION OR GROUP DISCUSSION

1. We have our plans. God has his. How do we discern one from the other? How can they intertwine?

2. Larry Thompson wrote:

Divine interruptions can bring new demands on an already difficult life. That's the very reason so many people ignore these God-given opportunities. They rationalize in the midst of their divine interruption, "I can't do one more thing. I am so busy right now. I have my own life to live. I don't need this crisis right now." Many people dismiss divine interruptions because they can't comprehend how they can reconcile this new demand on their life with their own plans.[9]

What can we do to overcome this tendency to ignore divine interruptions?

3. Tutuvi's sacrifices for her son, Dela, were very evident. What part of this true story did you find the most sacrificial? How does that compare with the sacrifices that we make for each other?

4. When were you blessed with a divine interruption that turned into a blessing?

5. I have learned to respect the African culture in that they often are quite willing to care for their own nieces or nephews. What can we learn from this?

6. Just yesterday, Tutuvi called me on the phone and sang a song to me. It was a song that had moved her heart that morning. I stopped, listened, and it touched my spirit as well. Little did she know that I was about to leave for a doctor's appointment. But listening to her testimony in song was more important to me than being on time for my appointment. The song was "I Will Run to You." What a lesson she taught me and continues to teach me. Can we really alter our schedules to just listen to a song, and forget our agenda when the clock keeps ticking? What really counts in life: the clock or listening to people's hearts?

*All the names in this chapter have been changed.

Chapter Nine

GOD, WHERE IS MY SISTER?

Scenes of the evacuation of American forces out of Saigon in April of 1975 are etched in my memory. I remember seeing television footage of one helicopter after another transporting people, gripped in panic, out of the city. And for those left behind, there was a feeling of doom.

The Do family ran through the streets during curfew, dodging bullets and explosives. Their only hope was to get themselves to the Saigon River that wound its way through the city. They had been told that a particular dock along the river held a "barge boat" that would take them out of the country. When they arrived at the dock, they saw some friends, which was a comfort. They jumped onto the barge boat—which turned out to be a commercial sailing vessel. Now safely on board, Yen and Duong Do opened up a package of two pounds of cooked rice and fed it to their three-year-old. Yen's sister, Yen, and Duong ate some themselves. This was the only food they had during the two-day voyage to the Philippine Islands. This barge was so crowded that they took turns standing while the others sat.

Yen and Duong Do were among the many Vietnamese who left their country. With their three-year-old daughter, Anhthu, and Yen's sister, Dzung, they sought a way of escape from Saigon. They had left Vietnam with only the clothes on their backs. The gold that they had put in their suitcases was stolen from them when they left the dock and went on the barge. The person who stole the gold was the very person who helped them get onto the barge.

Once the Do family arrived in the Philippines, they landed at Subic Bay, a US Navy base, where there was an abundance of American food specifically intended for Vietnamese refugees. They were given new clothes and stayed at the American base in the Philippines for the next three days, where the US Air Force was based during the Vietnam War.

Finally, the time came for them to leave the Philippines and take the long last leg of their journey to the United States. When they arrived in America, they went to a refugee camp in Arkansas and waited for an American sponsor. Accommodations were crowded: three families to one room and a single common washroom for an entire building. The beds were far from comfortable. That was their home for the next few months.

The Do family learned that a wealthy man from Colorado had offered to be their sponsor. He flew his own private plane to Arkansas and met them. They were advised, however, that it would be better to have a church sponsor them rather than an individual person. They decided to wait for a church. While they waited, Duong Do worked for the Red Cross as an interpreter. Soon the news came that the Elmhurst Christian Reformed Church in Illinois had offered to be their sponsor. They immediately accepted the offer, in spite of the fact that they had hoped to go to California, where many of their friends were living and the weather was more to their liking.

Ministry to Refugees

The modern refugee program in the United States is rooted in polices that came into being following the Vietnam War. These fell under the broad umbrella of the Refugee Act of 1980. Currently, the Bureau of Population, Refugees, and Migration (the State Department) and the Office of Refugee Resettlement (Department of Homeland Security) have been given the mandate of implementing the Refugee Act.

Since 1980, approximately 1.8 million refugees have been invited to live in the United States. Annual arrivals typically fall somewhere between forty thousand and seventy-five thousand people. Most arrive as family units—parents with their children.

Sponsorship is part of the process of resettlement in the United States. Refugees must have a sponsor (typically, a church or a para-church ministry) before they are permitted to leave a refugee camp. The sponsor helps ease the final transition into American culture. Sponsors are responsible for the refugees' first 180 days in the United States. Responsibilities of sponsors include:
- locating an apartment and paying the rent for one to three months;
- providing minimal furnishings for the apartment;

- purchasing food; and
- helping refugees obtain social security cards, school registration, health benefits, and so on.

I believe that churches are perfectly equipped to care for refugees. They are ready-made communities that have as their mandate the making of disciples among the peoples of the world (Matthew 28:19–20). Yet, in this case, rather than sending out missionaries, the peoples of the world are coming to them. What is more, refugees are in desperate need and are actively seeking sponsors. So the church has this opportunity to share the Word of God with people while loving them in a manner that is profoundly practical. "By this everyone will know that you are my disciples," Jesus said, "if you love one another" (John 13:35).

Of all of their needs, the greatest is love—God's love. When they see total strangers reaching out and loving them in ways that are far beyond normal, and they learn that these same people are worshippers of the one true God, this may be the first step toward their conversion to the Christian faith. The Holy Spirit, I believe, is pleased to draw people to a saving knowledge of Jesus Christ in this fashion.

Looking back on my childhood, I recall how often I felt alone except for a few special friends and some close cousins. When I reached my thirties, I came to believe that God had answered my childhood prayer by bringing me like-minded women, with whom I had grown close and who had become my spiritual sisters.

When Yen Do from Vietnam entered my life, I became close to her by caring for her daughter and helping her family settle into suburban life outside of Chicago. I helped her learn to speak English, along with other extended family members. The refugee committee from our church did an excellent job helping them with the resettlement process. My job was just simply to be their friend.

The Do family proved to be industrious people. Duong and Yen cleaned the Tri-City Bank at nighttime. During the day, Duong went to training to become a loan officer. Yen went to school at the College of DuPage, training for work in the government public aid program.

In a few months, Yen and I had become much more than friends. She became the sister I longed for as a child. We even gave birth to sons at approximately the same time. Yen gave birth to David, whose middle name is Elmhurst, because the Elmhurst Christian Reformed Church sponsored her family. I gave birth to Mark, our fifth child. Our boys grew up as brothers. In fact, when they each were married, they stood up in each other's wedding. David and Mark were the candle lighters when our oldest daughter, Mary, was married. This bond has continued to the present time. Now both of the Do's children, David and Anhthu, have children of their own. Anhthu is a neurologist, and David is a lawyer. To them, we are known as Uncle Ken and Aunt Jane. We share holidays, birthdays, baptisms, and the birthdays of our children and grandchildren. Thanksgiving is not complete without Aunt Yen's egg rolls.

In order for Ken and me to fully appreciate the culture of the Do family, we made a trip to Cambodia and Vietnam. As we walked the streets of Saigon, now called Ho Chi Minh City, I tried to imagine Yen and Duong living among these people. Never in our lives have we seen so many Buddha statues. But I praise God that Yen and Duong are Catholics who love the same Lord Jesus Christ as we do.

One of my goals in Vietnam was to enter into one of the tunnels that the Viet Cong used during the war.

We finally found one. It looked small and foreboding. I took a deep breath and said a quiet prayer: "Lord, though I am seventy years old, I am determined to do this. Help me." The tunnel was pitch dark, musty, and unusually warm. Down into the tunnel I went, crawling on my hands and knees. I followed the person ahead of me as closely as possible. When he turned a corner, I turned. Forty-five feet later, I emerged from the tunnel to greet Ken, who was waiting for me. The experience gave me an appreciation for the Vietnamese people who fought and lived in these tunnels as they waged war with the Americans. Three decades later, the door is open for Americans to visit this land and their people whom we now respect.

In Ho Chi Minh City, we found it difficult to perform the simplest of activities, such as crossing a street. The streets were crowded with motorcycles speeding along in both directions. It was even difficult to walk along the sidewalks because so many people were selling food in sidewalk stalls.

Although our cultures are so totally different—including the food, housing, transportation, and language—genuine love for a person sees the heart of an individual. The members of this Vietnamese family are people of integrity whom we really admire. Our ties with the Do family have helped our entire family respect and appreciate other cultures.

> **MEDITATION**
>
> If we believe that our prayer requests honor the Lord, we should not be so quick to drop them when the answers do not come within a few days or so. God answers prayer with either *yes, no,* or *wait.*
>
> *"Do not be anxious about anything, but in every situation by prayer and petition with thanksgiving, present your requests to God."* Philippians 4:6

Questions for Personal Reflection or Group Discussion

1. Does your church missionary board have the names and phone numbers of local government agencies whose responsibility is to implement the Refugee Act? Consider the blessings of sponsoring a refugee family. It can change your life forever. One such organization is Exodus International.

2. Do you know of anyone who has been involved in sponsoring a refugee? If yes, how did it go? Was it a positive or negative experience?

3. What role does our culture play in concern for refugees? What can be done to improve developing an awareness of refugees?

4. How can we encourage each other to get out of our comfort zones and include different cultures in our lives?

5. I have adopted daughters from Togo, Africa, and the Ukraine, and a sister from Vietnam, Pakistan, and Liberia. Our family has been blessed in every outreach adventure. Welcome others into your lives. I encourage you to think outside of the box and achieve the benefits of welcoming other races into your life. What nationality would you feel comfortable in embracing as part of your extended family?

6. How has God answered your prayer requests? Are you waiting patiently on the Lord?

Chapter Ten

A LITTLE LAMB

I met Danny over twenty years ago when I was serving as director of Little Lambs. It was Wednesday morning and time for Little Lambs to begin. Linda hurried to keep up with her little son as Danny ran into the church. "Hurry up, Mom," Danny called. "I want to do Play-Doh today." Danny loved Little Lambs.

He was a quiet, reserved, and never-disobedient three-year-old, but he had lots of energy, which would suggest that he was healthy. But he was not OK: he had been born with a heart murmur. At first the doctors told Linda and Gary not to be concerned, that the condition would likely correct itself. Then one day Linda noticed that his small chest was beginning to expand in a strange manner. An ultrasound and an angiogram were performed, and Linda and Gary learned that Danny had a hole in his heart. Open-heart surgery was the only remedy.

Though Linda had attended church as a child, as an adult, church had become little more than a Christmas and Easter event for her. She appreciated Little Lambs and the spiritual training it offered for her children, but her own spiritual life was dry and empty.

Linda and I were standing near the church kitchen when she broke the news to me that Danny would soon be having open-heart surgery. I relayed this information to the Little Lambs staff, and we all prayed for him.

About a week later, as Linda was pushing a grocery cart down the aisle of a grocery store near her home, she turned a corner and almost bumped into me. We stopped and talked. When I asked how Danny was doing, Linda opened up and tearfully poured out her heart. I listened and offered as many words of encouragement as I could.

Then, just before surgery, one of the teachers on staff reminded Linda that we were all seriously praying for Danny. This was an indication to Linda that we took a personal interest in her son in spite of the fact that we had many other children in the program.

The surgery was successful. Afterward, I went to Gary and Linda's home to see how Danny was doing. I brought a small gift and offered additional words of encouragement.

Linda continued to help out at Little Lambs, and several weeks later, after Danny returned to Little Lambs, Linda asked if she could be part of the program. Of course I said yes. She became a substitute teacher, filling in when needed. As she worked alongside the others in the program, she sensed a spirituality that was lacking in her own life. The teachers had a relationship with God that she did not have. Their love for Jesus was intense, much more real than it was in her life. Then she prayed and received Jesus Christ as her Savior and Lord. Two years later, little Danny did the same.

Several years later, Linda became one of our Bible teachers and then our Bible session coordinator. Together we chose the curriculum, visuals, and Bible verse for the month. She did this important job for at least fifteen years.

Reaching Little Ones for Christ

Little Lambs is an evangelistic ministry to preschool children ages three through six. God has enabled me to develop it from twenty-five students to over four hundred students over the past three decades. We currently have five sessions, and we value each child as a gift from God. During that time, the two hours are divided into five curriculum areas: music, crafts, Bible, creative learning, and free play. Recently, I passed the baton on to my dear friend. In our community, this is the place that preschool children love to attend.

Our purpose in Little Lambs is to present the Gospel of Jesus Christ in a manner that is meaningful to young minds and to lead preschoolers to the saving knowledge of Jesus Christ. Each year we see the Lord work in these little lives as they invite Jesus to be their Savior.

One of the ways we present the Gospel is through color association:
- Yellow represents heaven: Jesus is preparing a home for us. It is a gift that is not earned or deserved, but God in his mercy saved us. (John 14:1–3)
- Black represents sin. "For all fall short of the glory of God" (Romans 3:23).

- Red represents the blood of Jesus. "He himself bore our sins in his body on the cross" (1 Peter 2:24).
- White represents that we cleanse our heart from sin. "The blood of Jesus, his Son, purifies us from all sin" (1 John 1:7).
- Green represents spiritual growth that occurs when we listen to God's Word, talk to God in prayer, and worship him in a Bible-teaching church.

Every week, the children are encouraged to dress in the color that has been designated as the particular color for the week. This helps reinforce the Gospel message for the week.

Then we have Salvation Week, when the steps of salvation are reviewed and every child is asked individually if he or she would like to invite Jesus to live in his or her heart. During Salvation week, the angels in heaven rejoice because many children take this spiritual step in their lives. The parents are informed through a special card what their son or daughter has done that week. So the entire family is able to rejoice with the child.

TRAGEDY STRIKES

Years later, Danny, now called Dan, was a 20 year old student at Northern University. On Valentine's Day, Dan called his mother, Linda to wish her a Happy V Day. Just a few minutes later, Linda was working her nursing shift when the terrible call came at 2:30 p.m. Her former husband, Gary, told her that there had been a shooting at Northern University and that Dan was one of the victims. Linda rushed to Kishwaukee Hospital where she and Gary were granted permission to see Dan and say their final good byes.

In the meantime, Linda's second husband, Bob, stayed at their home praying with us and other friends from our Bible Study group, Bob's son and the pastor from his church. When Linda came home around midnight, we hugged and cried together.

Linda and Bob were in shock. All they knew was that they were on a spiritual journey that they did not ask to be on. They were on it and could not get off.

The following Sunday, Linda stood up at church and shared with the congregation her sorrow and thankfulness. Indeed, she was grieving over the loss of her son…but she was also thankful. She was thankful that Dan had received Christ as his Savior as a young child and that he rededicated his life to Christ as a young teenager. She knew that she would see her son again…in heaven.

One of the central reasons why we offer spiritual training to preschool children is that we do not know how long each person's life on this earth will last. Some people's lives reach well into their adult years. Others do not make it out of infancy. And in between these two age groups, many people's lives abruptly come to a conclusion.

Danny made it to his twentieth birthday. Yet we are thankful that he made a profession of faith in Jesus Christ and that his sins had been forgiven, cleansed by the blood of Jesus Christ who died in his place at the cross. That gave Linda, and all of the other Christians who knew Dan, a profound sense of peace at his funeral. In the midst of their tears was a steady and unshakeable confidence that they would see him again someday.

The Apostle Paul wrote that we do not "grieve like the rest of men, who have not hope." We believe that Jesus died and rose again, and so we believe that

God will bring with Jesus those who have fallen asleep [passed away] in him" (1 Thess. 4:13–14).

> **MEDITATION**
> *"For to me, to live is Christ and to die is gain"* (Phil. 1:21).

QUESTIONS FOR PERSONAL REFLECTION OR GROUP DISCUSSION

1. Giving one's life to the Lord is important at any age, but the younger a child does it, usually the stronger his or her foundation in Christ will be. What has been your experience with leading a person to salvation?

2. Whenever a child has a health problem and needs surgery like Danny, any parent would be very anxious. How can those fears be made less stressful?

3. Life is always too short, but especially when a person dies in youth. What does this teach us about life?

4. Mass murders have been too prevalent in our culture, whether they occur on college campuses, in schools, at shopping centers, marathons, or other public places. What are some of the causes of these events? What can we do as Christians to create a safer world for this generation and future generations?

5. What is our only comfort in death?

6. What is the best way to comfort the family of an innocent person who died by a tragic shooting or accident?

7. Have you ever been involved in a situation where an innocent person died from an accident? What advice do you have to share with others?

Chapter Eleven

BABY AT HER DOORSTEP

In the Little Lambs preschool program, our staff has encountered many children with unique needs and personalities. We have had a child with dwarfism, children with little knowledge of the English language, others were autistic, and many with learning disorders. Rarely has a child been turned away due to special needs. We always try our best to love each and every child that the Lord has brought our way.

This expression of love at Little Lambs included Jake.* He was three years old when he came to the program in 1988. His mother, Sharon, had high energy and was committed to the protection of her child at all costs. We assured her that her son, who had a cleft lip and a noticeable speech impediment, would be loved and treated the same as all of the children in the rest of the class—with the love of Jesus.

Sharon was pleased with the care and the religious training that her son was receiving. When he needed rides to Little Lambs, we would pick him up and then take him home. When Sharon's basement flooded after a hard rain, people from our church helped them with the repairs. Love has no limits.

After a few months, Sharon began to take a closer look at the Bible stories that Jake was learning. She thought that she would study what he was learning even though she was Roman Catholic and our church is Protestant. She joined Coffee Break, an interfaith Bible study for women, and the Word of God spoke to her heart.

During this time, Jake was growing in his faith, and so was Sharon. She saw Christian love in action when people helped each other. She joined our church. Following the church service, we had a party at our home to celebrate. Jake grew up in a home where his mother taught him about the Lord.

People from other Denominations

Anyone who knows anything about church history knows that the church has seen splits, divisions, and schisms. And this happens despite Jesus's words: "By this everyone will know that you are my disciples, if you love one another" (John 13:35).

Yet, those who criticize the church for its many divisions often overlook the doctrinal purity (the truth) that is foundational to the Christian faith. Many of the divisions within the church took place because people in high leadership swerved away from the Gospel of Jesus Christ and began preaching a false Gospel. We are instructed to turn away from these false prophets. The Apostle Paul said: "For such men are false apostles, deceitful workers, masquerading as apostles of Christ. And no wonder, for Satan himself masquerades as an angel of light" (2 Corinthians 11:13–14).

Since the sixteenth century, one of the major divisions within Christianity has been that of Roman Catholicism and Protestantism. Just down the street from my church is a large Roman Catholic Church, whose parking lot is full every Sunday, as this is also true of our church. Between these two churches, there is mutual interaction of two ministries, Little Lambs and Coffee Break Bible Study. We praise God for this mutual interest between the two churches.

I am certainly no theologian and am not prepared to make sweeping statements about the Roman Catholic Church in its entirety, from the Vatican on down. But this much I do know. I personally know Roman Catholics whose faith in Jesus Christ and whose understanding of the Gospel is the same as mine. I also know Roman Catholics who seemingly have no genuine faith whatsoever. For them, it is all a matter of ritual observance and church attendance; they haven't a clue as to a correct knowledge of the Gospel of Jesus Christ.

But then again, not everyone who attends my church is a true believer either. Every so often, I hear testimonies from someone who had been in attendance at our church for years and just finally received Christ as his or her Savior.

My point is this: We have to look at people as individuals, not as members of this or that church. Do they, or do they not, know Jesus Christ as their personal Savior? Are they attending a church where they are being fed with the truth from God's Word? Is their church vibrant, providing them with the needed support to grow in Christ, where the Holy Spirit is actively at work?

In the case of Sharon, she did not know Christ as her personal Savior. It was only through our Coffee

Break ministry that the Lord spoke to her and showed her the way out of spiritual darkness and into the glorious light of Jesus Christ. It only became natural, then—since she received Christ as Savior at Elmhurst Christian Reformed Church, and she developed friends there who taught her the fundamentals of Christian growth—for her to join ECRC.

Those in Sharon's family did not share her newfound faith in Jesus Christ. Her husband became heavily involved with alcohol, and her daughter, Joan, became a rebellious teen. At the age of sixteen, she was asked to leave the home. When she had no place to go, Ken and I invited Joan to stay with us. She stayed for a few weeks and then ran away. She lived with another family from our church and later a third family.

In time we learned that Joan was pregnant. After the baby was born, the big question was who would care for this baby girl? Even Joan realized she was not mature enough to raise a child. Volunteers at PADS (an evening shelter for the homeless), threatened to call DCFS because Joan was leaving the baby with male drug addicts while she was working during the day. After much prayer, two other members of our church, Tim and Nancy, agreed to temporarily care for baby Greta when she was six weeks old. Bringing a child like this into their home was not new to them. They had already adopted a child from South Korea.

Tim and Nancy went to the PADS shelter to see how Joan was doing. They always took Greta so Joan would have opportunities to bond with her child. But Joan was not interested in bonding with the baby.

What were Tim and Nancy to do? They already had four children of their own. Could they handle a fifth child? As they spent days in prayer, three events took place: someone dropped off diapers at their front door; another close friend wrote a large check to assist them with expenses if they decided to adopt the baby; and the Lord reminded Nancy that she said that she would never adopt another child unless God dropped one off at her front door.

They finally concluded that this was indeed the will of God for their lives. Following the adoption of Greta, Joan kept in touch with them for about seven years. Then she permanently turned away. Her world had become one of drugs and alcohol. She had no time for anything else, especially a child.

Years later, Tim and Nancy discovered that Greta suffered from a genetic mental illness. This resulted in numerous hours of professional counseling and changing of schools, adolescent homes, and boarding schools. In looking back, they said we have no regrets, but have learned to surrender it all to the Lord, remembering that God is in control. Greta is now well accepted in her new home and in the Christian community.

Once again, radical hospitality occurred because a family cared deeply and went above and beyond to involve their lives in someone else's. Then, as believers in the Lord, the families within the church supported them. Caring for each other in this way is what the family of God is all about.

MEDITATION

"Do nothing out of selfish ambition or vain conceit. Rather, in humility value others above yourselves, not looking to your own interests but each of you to the interests of the others" (Phil. 2:3–4).

QUESTIONS FOR PERSONAL REFLECTION OR GROUP DISCUSSION

1. How do you as an individual or as a church support families who have children with deformities or disabilities?

2. What was the result of giving God's love to Sharon and Jake? How did it impact Joan?

3. Have you ever put your fleece (Judges 6:36-39) before the Lord, and have you seen it fulfilled?

4. Loving special needs children is part of what it means to enfold the flock. How did the Holy Spirit bless all the people involved in the ministry to Sharon, Jake, and Greta?

5. Has anyone you know involved himself or herself in the ministry of a special needs child? What were the positive benefits? What were the challenges?

6. Every child is a gift from God. We tend to value someone's life based on the quality of life that he or she is capable of living. Yet we need to accept all people as God created them. I am speaking to myself. We have experienced this in our family. I keep on asking the Lord, "What do you have to teach me in this experience?" He has taught me so much, and I will never be the same person. Can you apply this to your life? How has it affected you?

*All the names in this chapter have been changed.

Chapter Twelve

SPIRITUAL WARFARE

In 1993, Pastor Bert De Jong challenged the ministerial staff of my church to write down goals for our lives for the next few decades. I was fifty-two years old at the time, and my goal for the next decade of my life was to reach out to orphans. I was inspired by the verse from the Epistle of James: "Religion that God our Father accepts as pure and faultless is this: to look after orphans and widows in their distress and to keep oneself from being polluted by the world" (James 1:27).

Throughout my life, this verse had always captured my heart. Now was the time for me to put it into practice. I asked the Lord to show me the way to reach out to the orphans in our world.

My husband came home from work with an article from the *Chicago Tribune* in 1995 about a Little Lambs camp in the Ukraine. His business partner's wife, Kathy, worked with me on the craft committee for Little Lambs at church and was curious when she saw this article. It was a ministry that specialized in caring for orphans. Because our ministries shared the same name, I made a call. I spoke with Renate Kurtz, who is the president of the Summer Ministry to orphans in the Ukraine but who lives in the United States. At the conclusion of the call, she asked if we could get together and talk in person. I invited her over to my home for lunch.

As Renate explained this ministry to me, I sensed the Holy Spirit speaking to my heart, telling me that this was for me. She explained to me that the ministry would involve crafts and telling Bible stories through an interpreter or via pantomime. I believed that with puppets on a stage, biblical stories could be presented to the children in an entertaining and compelling fashion.

With my husband's blessing, the desire of my heart was met in 1995. In a few months, my friend Carol and I were off to the Ukraine.

OFF TO LOVE ORPHANS IN THE UKRAINE

When our airplane landed in Kiev, our team of seven was ushered to a rusty old orange truck. The suitcases were thrown onto the bed of the truck. We climbed aboard—also onto the back of the truck—and off we went.

Our suitcases served as our seats for the trip. Sitting backward in the bed of this bouncy truck was a serious problem for me as I suffer from motion sickness. As the truck traveled down the road, we didn't know where we were going or how long it would take to get to our destination. Thirty minutes, an hour, two hours, half a day…we hadn't a clue. We also didn't know how to tell the driver when we needed a washroom break. He spoke Ukrainian. We saw only a few gas stations alongside the road, and most of them were dirty and did not appear to have restrooms.

Mile after mile, the truck traveled south. We remained quiet, keeping our thoughts to ourselves. As I looked at the faces of the others on the team, I saw bewildered expressions. I am sure that my expression was no different. In the pit of my stomach, I had a sick sense of doom—that we were being transported to a concentration camp or some such place.

After four and a half hours, we arrived at our destination: Pereyaslv, the location of Orphanage 21. It was nestled in a forest by the Napier River.

We stepped down from the truck, stretched our legs, and took a wide look at what would be our home for the next thirty days. The orphanage had two hundred children with no parents to love and guide them. People were hired by the state to watch over them and teach them during the school year. But did they love them? Did they care about their emotional struggles? And what about their spiritual struggles? Did they even know that such struggles existed?

Conditions at the Orphanage

We quickly learned that some of the children at the orphanage were mentally challenged. Some were autistic, a few had been diagnosed with attention deficit hyperactivity disorder, and others had been born with fetal alcohol syndrome. Mixed in this group were children who had no apparent disorders other than chronic bitterness, bewilderment and sadness.

The children lived on a diet of cheese, bread, potatoes, buckwheat and soup. Occasionally, small pieces of chicken or pork were added to the soup. I had been warned that the meals would be deficient in protein, so I had brought a large tub of peanut butter that I kept in my bedroom.

If we wanted fresh water, we had to pump it from a nearby spring. Showers were nonexistent. To wash, we went with our swimming suits and a bar of soap to the Napier River a few hundred yards to the north of the orphanage. When we went to retrieve our towel to dry off, we wiped the algae and slime that had been floating on the river from our bodies and swimsuits.

We observed that the children feared many of the social workers and teachers at the orphanage. When they acted up in school, they were beaten with a large stick. And if they continued to act up, they were sent to the "crazy school." It was located a few miles from the orphanage and was, I was told, a mental hospital. At the "crazy school," the orphans were given sedatives that put them into a drug-induced stupor, which, in turn, kept them pacified. Six weeks later, they would return to the orphanage. If they acted up again, they would be beaten or sent to the "crazy school" again. We watched all this with horror and dismay yet were mindful to keep our thoughts to ourselves. We were guests at the orphanage. We too had rules we were required to follow.

At age eighteen all orphans were discharged from the orphanage. Many, we were told, went to the streets and lived as prostitutes, drug traffickers, or gangsters. Some of them went to trade schools to learn to cook or paint.

The entire ministry team sensed an oppressive spirit hovering over the orphanage. We remained in a constant state of prayer—for ourselves as well as for the orphans, the social workers and the teachers.

Our ministry at the orphanage was to provide the children with love. Throughout the month, we told a series of Bible stories through a translator. We used puppets and flannel graphs as visual aids, with staff acting out the stories as a supplement. The children were attentive. When the story time was over, they made friendship bracelets. And, of course, we all played games together. From morning to night, we loved them unconditionally. The children yearned to be hugged.

One day we were told that government inspectors were coming to check on the camp and see what we were doing with the children. We took out our best crafts and had them on display. More importantly, we did not hide our true agenda, which was to share the Gospel of Jesus Christ with the children. The inspectors said nothing negative to us, so we assumed that everything was OK with them.

When our month at the orphanage came to an end, we left with broken hearts. We had fallen in love with all the children. At our farewell, tears swelled in the children's eyes as well as ours. Some of the children took large rocks and lined them across the road so our bus could not leave the orphanage. Finally, after much persuasion, they removed the rocks. On the return trip to Kiev, we sat in silence. We were going back to a land of wealth, but these children were being left behind.

THREE SPECIAL GIRLS

Since that first visit to the Ukraine, I have returned fourteen times. Through the many visits, the Spirit of God has drawn my heart in a special way to these orphans. On my second trip, we were taken to a different orphanage, but two girls that I had grown to love at Orphanage 21—Luba Kovenko and Cheeta—had been transferred to this new orphanage. I believe this was an act of God. This way, we could build on our previous ministry with these girls.

Because Luba could speak a little English, I knew something about her past. Her mother had been committed to a mental hospital, and her father was an alcoholic.

During my second visit to the Ukraine, Luba repented of her sins and received Jesus Christ as her Lord and Savior. To this day, she refers to me as her mother. Several years later, Ken and I decided to provide financially for her when she enrolled at the University of Kiev. She has since graduated and is now a professor of English. Each time I returned to the Ukraine, I met Luba at the Little Lambs office. It was "reunion time" year after year. I have also met her grandmother and her sister with two children. We often e-mail each other. She is one of my adopted daughters from the Ukraine.

At Orphanage 21, Cheeta was one of the toughest of the orphans. Her hair was bleached blonde, and her stride was like that of a demanding boy. Others told me that she swore constantly and was not the least bit interested in anything spiritual. Unlike many of the other orphans, she refused to be touched. Hugging was therefore out of the question. By my third visit to the Ukraine, however, her heart had changed. It finally struck her that our love for her was genuine. Why else would we keep coming back, year after year?

Cheeta received Jesus Christ as her Lord and Savior. The Spirit of God transformed her hard, bitter exterior into a soft, gentle spirit. She began talking of Jesus Christ openly and often. She began to help the other Christian Ukrainian leaders. Her heart's desire was to go to Africa and be a missionary. She received her training through YWAM (Youth With A Mission). She went to Africa and cared for babies suffering from

AIDS. A year and a half after that, she felt the Spirit of God calling her to receive further Bible training. She went to Cambodia and studied at a Bible college, and later she became a teacher at the same school. She has now returned to the Ukraine to become director of a house for orphans, the Beehive. To Cheeta, I am Aunt Jane.

In November of 2012, Ken and I took a trip to Cambodia where we met Cheeta, also known as Sasha, who was then teaching Bible studies in Cambodia. I traveled halfway around the world to meet her, and she traveled by bus for four hours so we could share the bond that began when she was thirteen. I waited and waited in front of our hotel, praying that she would show up. Finally, there she was, riding on a motorcycle. What a reunion! We could not stop talking about everything that had transpired in our lives over the past few years. She was wearing the Bulls T-shirt that I had given her two years before. I had a few articles of clothing from the United States I thought she would wear in the hot, humid weather in Cambodia. One of our main reasons for traveling to Cambodia was to meet Cheeta. However, the only contact we had for arranging this meeting was my e-mail telling her what hotel we would be staying at in Siem Ream. Our dreams were fulfilled. Only our sovereign God could arrange such a reunion!

About five years after I met Cheeta in the orphanage, the Holy Spirit drew my heart to another orphan, a girl named Luba, with the same last name as my previously "adopted" daughter. Luba had five siblings, and all of them were put into the orphanage system with no knowledge of their parents. Yet each one was placed in a different orphanage. Since they kept on telling the directors of the various orphanages that they had brothers and sisters, an effort was put forth to seek out where the siblings might be, and eventually they ended up together. What a time of rejoicing that was for the children. Now, four of the five siblings have received Jesus Christ as their Lord and Savior.

After my second Luba Kovenko graduated from the University of Kiev, she became a preschool teacher. She met a young man, Sergie, to whom she was attracted, yet he was not a Christian. Since I was the only mother that she had ever known, she wrote to me asking for my advice. I told her that the only way their relationship would work was if he received Christ as his Savior.

Sergei began joining Luba at their youth group and became quite involved. A few months later, he received Jesus Christ as his Savior. They were engaged. Luba sent me e-mail! "I have a dream that my mother would be at my wedding." This touched my heart. So the day after we had a big Thanksgiving dinner with our family, we left the United States and flew to the Ukraine. Luba had arranged for someone to meet us at the airport and drive us to Rivne. What a long, scary trip that was! It was late at night, and we had a teenage fellow drive us to our destination, the Beehive, where many of the orphans live. When we opened the door on that cold winter night, there was my daughter. We hugged and cried together. I had a most special gift for her to wear on her wedding night: a satin gown that I bought for her in the United States.

She was married in a Baptist church in Rivne. It is the custom for the mothers to give the couple away, which meant that Sergei's mother and I had to pray during the service and each give our child to be married. Sergei's family was responsible for the food, and the children in the Beehive provided the decorations and entertainment. Ken and I will never forget this wedding.

Chapter Twelve

Three years later, the Lord blessed Sergei and Luba with a baby girl, Solomia. It was a privilege to send hundreds of diapers in a container to the Ukraine for my adopted grandchild. A picture of her now appears on a ledge in our family room along with photos of all our other grandchildren. During the summer of 2012, I saw my first Ukrainian grandchild, Solomia. Even though we have twenty-three grandchildren of our own, she too is special to me.

DOING CHORES IN THE ORPHANAGES

On yet another one of my trips to the Ukraine, many orphans received Christ as their Savior. It was a most exciting time. Sadly, the director of the Ukrainian camp did not appreciate the spiritual atmosphere. Yet, without any hesitation, we continued with our plans for the orphans. We entertained the orphans with games and had fun doing creative crafts with them. They loved the humorous skits and Bible dramas. However, the director resented the fact that the children showed so much affection and love toward the Americans—and not to the Ukrainian teachers.

To make things more difficult, the director insisted that the children had to complete all their chores before they had their Bible lesson with us. So, as a staff, we decided that we would assist the children with their chores. One of the most ridiculous chores was picking up leaves that had fallen from the trees during the previous night. We had to do this by hand—that's right; they provided us with no rakes! We got on our hands and knees and helped them pick up the leaves.

On another day, we had to pick up the cottonwood fibers that had fallen from the trees overnight. Once again, we were on our hands and knees. We made a game out of it by seeing who would collect the most fibers and make the largest pile of cottonwood.

The chore that seemed most unreasonable was picking up the garbage that fell to the ground from the garbage truck. To us the reasonable thing would be to empty the garbage truck each night. That did not happen. The pickup truck was filled higher and higher. Every night, the wind blew and scattered the garbage on the ground. Even worse, the truck was parked near the pigpen where the odor was almost unbearable. Our goal was for the children to hear their Bible lesson and not to allow the chores to stand in the way of giving them the opportunity to hear the Word of God. So we assisted them, and they heard the Bible stories.

During these two weeks, we had a very godly translator, a young woman named Nina Ognivchuk. She represented the Americans so well to the Ukrainian director that the director could not help but see the improvement in the children's behavior and their love for the Lord.

Nina then asked two of the boys who accepted Christ if they would like to spend a few weeks at her home in August. They were very excited to have an opportunity to be in someone's home rather than in an orphanage run by the state. The director gave Nina permission to take Misha and Sergei to her home. Their stay was shortened because the state inspector was coming to the orphanage. Sergei and Misha had to be immediately returned to the orphanage so that everyone who was registered would be present when the inspector arrived.

Nina's parents lived in Shepetivka, Ukraine, which was about a ten-hour trip by car from the orphanage. During the boys' stay at their home, they saw potential in Misha and loved him as their own son. Without telling him, they began filing papers to adopt Misha.

Chapter Twelve

They did not have the finances to do this on their own, so Ken and I were pleased to assist them in the adoption process. Months later in the spring, they told Misha they were going to legally adopt him. Needless to say, he was overjoyed.

The Ognivchuk family is a large family with four sons and three daughters. Their father is a pastor whose salary is modest. He supplements this income by digging wells. Why take on another son? They believed it was God's will to help an orphan. Adopting Misha meant that two of their own sons had to move out and live in another flat, because the state had certain requirements for every family that adopted a child—Misha needed to have his own room.

After about six months, Misha seemed somewhat depressed. He acknowledged that he desired to find his biological parents and siblings. He wanted to know his roots.

Pastor Ognivchuk was very wise. He told Misha that he would make an effort to find Misha's biological family. Pastor Ognivchuk knew that Misha might leave them after all the effort they had made to adopt him, but Pastor Ognivchuk knew how much this meant to Misha, so he started the search. After detailed research, they found the village where Misha's parents might live. They located Misha's biological parents, and it was a touching moment when they met face-to-face. They hugged each other, and Misha also met his older brothers for the first time. His mother apologized over and over for taking Misha to the orphanage when he was a very young boy. To Misha's surprise, his mother told him that it would be much better for him to stay with Nina's family. There he had a future, and he was learning good values.

Misha's heart was torn: where did he really belong? If he stayed with his biological family, they might accept Christ as their Savior. He went back with the Ognivchuk family and prayed about it. After a few months of indecision, God spoke to his heart, and he decided to stay with the family that had adopted him.

Currently, Misha is attending a local college to become an artist. By e-mail, I have seen some of his artwork. He is an exceptional artist. As this story is written, I ask you to keep Misha in your prayers. Pray that he matures in his faith and uses his gifts to bring glory to God.

EXTENDING THE BLESSING

Every trip to the Ukraine is unique because it involves different children and new experiences. For my first eleven years there, I had never taken any of my immediate family members with me. However, in 2010, I took my fifteen-year-old granddaughter, Hope, with me. She is a reserved, beautiful, athletic girl who felt called by God to serve in the Ukraine. Who was I to question God's calling? Sometimes I think that only the orphans are changed on our mission trips. Not true. God changes all of us, especially those being sent to serve in God's name.

Before we left O'Hare Airport, Hope's large jar of peanut butter was removed from her carry-on by airport security. This was what she was planning to survive on while in the Ukraine because their food has very little protein. Not only did she have her peanut butter taken away, but also when we arrived at the orphanage, the mice nibbled the food that she had brought from home. Hope slept in a room with six Ukrainian girls, who were in hysterics over the mice eating their food.

Nothing stopped Hope's desire to reach out and touch the lives of the orphans. She returned to

Novomirgorod two years later with one of her cousins, Sam, and my daughter, Mary, who was creative and such an asset to the team. Our mission has become a family mission of three generations. That year, I was head leader of the team, which meant additional responsibilities. However, with the help of my family, it was no problem.

Passing the ministry on to my grandchildren has become one of my overall goals. In 2012, my grandsons, Devon Loerop and Matt Steenwyk, joined me. My grandsons were well respected by the Ukrainian boys because of their soccer skills. Matt's mother, my daughter, Mary, who now was experienced, joined me with another son, Sam Steenwyk. He played many of the Ukrainian songs on his guitar. They combined a Christian lifestyle with top-notch sport skills to relate to the orphans. Once again, it was three generations reaching out to orphans. What memories!

Resisting Spiritual Oppression

Spiritual oppression is genuine. When Christians walk into a geographical area where evil spirits have had the freedom to cross over and influence affairs in the physical realm, they instantly recognize it. Its most obvious manifestation is an inexplicable spiritual confusion. Where everything was once clear and orderly in their minds, now their spirits are struggling, almost as if they are gasping for spiritual air. A feeling of despair is another symptom. Scripture refers to it as:

- an inexplicable fear (1 Sam. 16:14);
- a spiritual blindness (2 Cor. 4:3–4; 11:3–4);
- an inability to engage in meaningful ministry (1 Thess. 2:18); and
- a sensation that one is under assault—that invisible fiery arrows are being shot in one's

direction (Eph. 6:16) or that he or she has been caught in a spiritual snare and is unable to break free (2 Tim. 2:26).

When we first arrived at Orphanage 21, we felt an oppressive spirit. We knew the answer was to double-check and make sure that we had our spiritual armor in place. This armor is:

- the belt of truth (Eph. 6:14a);
- the breastplate of righteousness (Eph. 6:14b);
- the Gospel of peace (Eph. 6:15);
- the shield of faith (Eph. 6:16);
- the helmet of salvation (Eph. 6:17a); and
- the sword of the Spirit, which is the Word of God (Eph. 6:17b).

And this we did. With this armor in place, we held our ground and prayed aggressively in the power of the Spirit (Eph. 6:14-18).

A group of 5 or 6 boys in the orphanage came up to the American and Ukrainian leaders, and said that they couldn't sleep. Every night when they we went to bed and closed their eyes, they would see cats pacing back and forth from wall to wall and they were terrified. After hearing this story repeated for a few days, a group of Christian leaders prayed over these boys. They prayed that the evil one who is giving these boys bad dreams be cast out of their minds. The next morning, the boys came up to the leaders with smiles on their faces and said that they slept well and did not see any cats. What an answer to prayer.

We were confident that God would answer our prayers and he did. We knew that we would see results. The Spirit of God did have victory over the evil spirits and take their domain from the orphans, bringing many them to faith in Jesus Christ.

As we waited, we leaned on two promises in Scripture. The first one said: "We demolish arguments and every pretension that sets itself up against the knowledge of God, and we take captive every thought to make it obedient to Christ" (2 Cor. 10:5). The second one said: "The one who is in you is greater than the one who is in the world" (1 John 4:4).

In each and every Bible lesson, we presented "the Gospel of peace" to the children, grounding all that we said were truths found in the Word of God. And we taught these teachings with a loving spirit—from morning until night. We hugged the children often.

A Crisis of Denial

In the West, and in much of the Second World (such as the Ukraine), many people are living in a massive crisis of denial. The realm of the spirit is put down, and the realm of secularism is lifted up. For them, religion is myth—a fable. And spiritual oppression, as I have been discussing in this chapter, is folklore.

I am convinced that they are attempting to replace the mystery of humankind's relationship with God with psychological explanations. Years ago, Karl Marx wrote that religion is the opium of the people. Years later, the leaders in the Soviet Union worked hard to help their people kick the habit. They maintained with the abolition of religion, the way would be paved for the establishment of a true happiness and contentment in society. Did it work? Of course not.

The absence of religion has left these people morally bankrupt. The constant beating that I witnessed in the orphanages and the commonly applied remedy of placing these children into drug-induced stupors so that they would become pacified is a horror beyond words. That was the level of child-rearing and school discipline to which these leaders in the orphanages had sunk. They failed to see that these children were made in the image of God and should be treated as such.

In all the orphanages that I visited, it was common to see children suffering from fetal alcohol syndrome, and I've been told that FAS is pandemic throughout all the orphanages in the Ukraine. What does that tell us? Are people self-medicating themselves with alcohol as a way of avoiding life? Do they not see the consequences of their alcoholism in their own lives as well as in the lives of their children?

I was not surprised to learn that Philip Yancey had come to similar conclusions. In 1991, he was part of a delegation of nineteen Christians who visited the former Soviet Union. In one of his books he said, "Wherever we went, government officials and private citizens alike affirmed that the true crisis in their nation was moral and spiritual. We heard that opinion expressed so adamantly and so often that I came to see it as the great untold story of Russia."[10] And, as far as I am concerned, you can add: it is also the great-untold story of the Ukrainian orphanages.

The absence of religion has left these people spiritually vulnerable. All of us in the ministry teams sensed a spiritual oppression hovering over all the orphanages that we visited. Is it possible that this is due to the efforts in the Ukraine to institutionalize atheism throughout the nation? The Bible states that when people refuse to acknowledge God or give thanks to him, he will give them over to a darkened mind (Rom. 1:21). And once this happens, a door is opened to a darkened spiritual oppression.

But this oppression is not all-powerful. It can be broken, and it has been. The testimony of those orphans who turned to Jesus Christ, trusting in him as their Lord and Savior, gives ample evidence of this. Their transition from darkness to light was so stark and undeniable that it showed the weakness of evil spirits to hold people in their grip. Luba Kovenko, Cheeta, Misha, and many others are testimonies that the darkness in the Ukraine, though powerful in its hold on people's souls, is no match for the power of the Spirit of God and the Word of God.

The absence of religion has caused many leaders in the Ukraine to ask Christians to come to their nation and reintroduce religion to their people. The ministry teams I have been a part of have been invited to come to the Ukraine over and over again. These leaders too have seen the changes in people's lives due to religion, and they yearn for more of it. So even though the orphanages are officially secular, many officials turn a blind eye when we preach the Gospel to the children and pass out Bibles.

Philip Yancey had the same experience during his visit to Russia. He wrote:

> *Almost overnight Russia moved away from an official position of atheism and hostility to become perhaps the most open mission field in the world. Wherever we went, officials invited us to set up exchange programs, relief efforts, study centers, and religious publishing ventures. The Russian leaders voiced a fear of total collapse and anarchy unless their society could find a way to change at the core.*[11]

Ironically, he added, it was due to the lobbying efforts of the Russian Orthodox Church that many of the restrictions against religion were reinstated.

Here in the United States of America, a nation that was founded upon Christian principles and where in its early days worship services were conducted in the Capitol on Sundays, we work hard to keep our secular institutions free of religion.

Listen once again to Philip Yancey: "Russian leaders seemed far more receptive to Christian influence than, say, their counterparts in the United States."[12]

The secularists in the United States want to take us to where the Ukraine and other parts of the former Soviet Union have been, while the Ukraine and other parts of the Soviet Union are now in search of the spirituality that the United States once took for granted.

> **MEDITATION**
> Once a person takes the ministry of heartfelt hospitality seriously, he/she can expect to engage in spiritual warfare. Yet the victory is ours because God is greater than all the forces of darkness.

QUESTIONS FOR PERSONAL REFLECTION OR GROUP DISCUSSION

1. If Satan is a defeated foe, why do we still have to confront him and battle with him?

2. Showing love toward those held in the grip of Satan is exhausting work. In what ways did the ministry team show love to the orphans even in the midst of obstacles?

3. Describe your experiences in reaching out to the unsaved. Have you experienced spiritual warfare?

4. Have you ever thought about passing on generational blessings to your family? If so, how can that be achieved?

5. Have you ever thought of doing a mission project as a family? Going to a food pantry? Serving in another country as a family? It can change your life and the lives of future generations. We need to consider how we can change from just being a moneymaking society into a society that strives to make a difference in the world for the Lord. May you be encouraged to make this a priority in your life.

Chapter Thirteen

THE STING OF BETRAYAL

Frequently, meeting the needs of people starts out with bringing groceries to their home. Helping out the August family in this way was quite convenient for us, since they lived only two miles from our home.

At our first visit, Judy told us that the night before, her husband, Marvin, had come close to committing suicide in the basement.* He smashed the bottom off a whiskey bottle with the intent of using it to commit suicide. A quick, deep slice, he reasoned, and it would be over. But he couldn't do it. After a few moments of contemplation, he put the sharp piece of glass down and decided to admit himself into a rehab hospital for alcoholics. After we heard this story, we asked to speak with Marvin, but it wasn't possible. He had already admitted himself to the hospital earlier that morning.

Marvin remained in the program, however, for only about half the treatment. After several weeks in the program, he made a vow to God to never touch another drop of alcohol, and figured that he was cured. And, to his credit, he kept that vow.

To our surprise, the Sunday after his release from the hospital, we met both Judy and Marvin at our church. They were a charming, attractive family with three beautiful children.

Since Judy was a Christian, we started to have a Bible study together once a week. She grew in her faith by leaps and bounds. We would choose a theme verse that we memorized. We both enjoyed and looked forward to our time together each week—we shared Scripture and prayer, and talked of family concerns. Then both Martin and Judy came together to the Bible study. It was wonderful to see them grow spiritually together.

They became good friends of ours. They were in our home numerous times, and we went on several vacations together. They even lived with us for a time when the "Great Flood of 1987" hit the western suburbs of Chicago. Marvin, who had been out of town, had a hard time believing me when I said that we sent his wife and three children down the street in a canoe. Marvin became involved with us in ministering to another family whose husband was an alcoholic.

THE KISS OF JUDAS

As I have mentioned repeatedly, ministry always involves an element of risk, because the people with whom we are ministering often come to us with a lot of baggage in their lives. We minister to them nonetheless, trusting that God will protect and care for us—come what may.

However, there are times when disappointment comes. Those to whom we pour out our love sometimes betray us. Judas Iscariot comes to mind as perhaps the most well-known example of this. "Judas," said Jesus at the moment of his arrest, "are you betraying the Son of Man with a kiss?" (Luke 22:48). Indeed, he did.

In the Old Testament, King David experienced a version of this wrenching kiss. His own son Absalom led an insurrection against David's kingdom, betraying him. Not only that, Ahithophel, David's trusted counselor, joined Absalom in this ill-fated insurrection (2 Sam. 15:12). "Even my close friend, whom I trusted, he who shared my bread," David later remarked, "has lifted up his heel against me" (Ps. 41:9).

Betrayal hurts. I venture to guess that every Christian minister who has ever served God has personally received some version of "the kiss of Judas." It seems to come with the territory.

In spite of Marvin's sobriety, he and his wife struggled with a number of problems—one of which was their financial situation. Because of his previous lifestyle with alcohol, they were deeply in debt.

One day, Judy confided to me: "The bank is going to foreclose on our home." We were both in tears, crying out to God to please intervene and not allow this to happen. Marvin was friendly, outgoing, and could win the confidence of anyone's heart. So when this spread around the church, a group of businessmen pooled their money together to help Judy and Marvin save their home. And, praise be to God, their home was saved.

Marvin was a remodeling contractor and had come up with a mixture of ingredients that made an exceptionally hard roofing tile that could potentially corner a large portion of the roofing tile market in

California and Mexico. He had secured funds from a wealthy investor out east to help produce the tile. He also talked to my husband, Ken, and convinced him to invest in the product. He showed us photos and other documentation that made the case that everything was on the up-and-up. We would get a percentage of the returns once this investment began to turn a profit.

Then, a few months later, while Ken was on one of his business trips to Mexico, he stopped over in Arizona to pay a visit to the plant where these tiles were being produced. To Ken's surprise, Marvin showed him nothing but an empty barn. It had all been a hoax.

Immediately, Ken demanded that he return his investment money. Marvin assured him that he would return the money, and the major portion was returned. Then, unexpectedly, Marvin and Judy moved out of Illinois. After several years, we received a phone call from Judy and a Christmas card. But the relationship had clearly ended, and the money was never completely returned. Attempts were made through Christmas cards to get in contact, but nothing was permanent. If they should appear at my doorstep today, we would welcome them warmly. One cannot keep a grudge, knowing how much Christ has forgiven us. Pray with us that this event will someday come.

MEDITATION

"Bear with each other and forgive one another, if any of you has a grievance against someone. Forgive as the Lord forgave you" (Colossians 3:13).

Chapter Thirteen

QUESTIONS FOR PERSONAL REFLECTION OR GROUP DISCUSSION

1. Developing relationships with Christians, whether they are raised in the church or newly converted, needs to be valued and respected. New Christians might lack moral maturity, but do we ever put limits on our involvement with them?

2. We must remember that God is the ultimate judge. To what extent are we discerning in our judgments against others?

3. Is it ever worth losing a friendship over money?

4. Discernment was lacking in this situation; however, it was hard to come to a conclusion concerning their honesty because the August family made every effort to help another family that was struggling with the use of alcohol. Our hearts ruled over wisdom. Where should we have drawn the line?

5. Looking back, legal advice should have been sought. When difficult decisions are made, should we decide with our mind or our heart or both?

6. If this had happened to you, would you still welcome the August family into your home?

7. What would Christ do?

*All the names in this chapter have been changed.

Chapter Fourteen

A Desperate Call

Throughout my life, words of inspiration have come to me from a variety of sources. The Bible, of course, is on the top of my list. Near the top are Christian friends who have shared their insights and ministry ideas with me, some of which have helped me better understand the gentle whispers from the Holy Spirit in my own life. A third area where the Lord has spoken to me is through Christian literature.

It was suggested that the small groups in our church read the book, *The Hole in Our Gospel* by Richard Stearns. While reading the book, I sensed the Holy Spirit speaking to me in one of the sentences: "It's not what you believe that counts," Richard Stearns said, "it's what you believe enough to do."[13]

After reading the first three chapters of this book, God put me to the test. I received a phone call from the Department of Child and Family Services. A social worker told me that a family from Africa was homeless, living in temporary quarters on the south side of Chicago. They were in need of a more permanent place to stay. I said to the lady: "I'll pray about it for a few days. I will then call you back."

After praying and sharing this request with my husband, I called DCFS and found out that the husband was a pastor and that the couple had a daughter. I learned that they were from Liberia and had won a lottery ticket to come to America, but they were still in need of an American sponsor and a place to stay.

I asked if I could pray with Evelyn, the mother of the family. When we prayed on the phone together, I knew she was a sister in Christ. How could I not welcome her? Our hearts became one. This was the beginning of a new relationship for both of our families.

Pastor Paul, Evelyn, and their daughter Angel were brought to our church by the social worker the third week in January 2011. They were all wearing African clothing. I went with outstretched arms to meet them. After church, they came to our home for dinner, and told many stories about what life was like while they were waiting for help to arrive.

Liberia was a nation established as an American colony in 1821. The idea was to send back to Africa those who had formerly been slaves. Since they had originally been taken from Africa, correcting this crime meant restoring them to their African homeland. Many esteemed American politicians were in favor of this return of the slaves to Africa, including Thomas Jefferson, James Madison, James Monroe, Henry Clay, Daniel Webster, John Randolph, and Abraham Lincoln.

Chapter Fourteen

Before the Civil War, thousands of freed slaves were repatriated to Liberia, whose name means "country of freedom."

Liberia became a free nation, with the blessings of the United States of America, in 1847. Its capital city was named Monrovia, in honor of President James Monroe. But Liberia struggled as a nation. Dictators took control of the government, and the people found themselves in bondage once again—this time to African masters. In the twentieth century, Communism took hold in that unfortunate land, in the wake of extreme poverty.

When the opportunity came to leave Liberia and find a new home in the United States of America, Paul, Evelyn, and Angel were anxious to come. Paul and Evelyn wanted their daughter Angel to have a better life and a good education. They sold all their earthly possessions, including their car, to purchase the airfare. That still did not get them enough money, so they had to borrow money from a friend at 100 percent interest that they were required to pay back within six months after they arrived.

Before we met Paul, he had been doing volunteer work for a community on the south side of Chicago, escorting children across the street as they went to and from school. It was dangerous work because the corner where he volunteered was a known gang area. People had been shot almost daily in this area. While he guided the children, he would pray to God to keep them safe. He prayed: "Dear Lord, send someone our way to help us out of this seemingly hopeless situation."

It had been extremely cold that December, and coming from a warm climate in Africa caused the cold weather in Chicago to seem even worse. At times, he felt that his feet were so totally frozen that they were about to fall off.

Once again, Ken and I took the risk of hosting a family in our home until we were able to find an apartment for them. What a fun afternoon my friend Diane and I had when we found an apartment for them. Diane, being in the real estate business, knew the way around our town and where rental buys existed.

Before we knew it, we were signing a contract for Paul, Evelyn, and Angel. Even though it was just a one-bedroom apartment, it was a place to call home. Within a week, friends in the church helped furnish the apartment. We were also grateful for the role that the deacons played in supporting us with their assistance.

After a few months, the family was blessed to be accepted in the Bridges program, which assisted with their rent. They were given mentors, Kyle and Sherri, who were not only mentors but also good friends.

Will Paul, Evelyn, and Angel ever return to their homeland? It is Paul's dream to be educated as a chaplain in the United States and apply it to his culture to help his people. He would like to complete the orphanage he started in Liberia. Lord willing, this dream will be fulfilled. As for us, we have gained another brother, sister, and niece.

As Christians, we need to avail ourselves of good Christian literature—both fiction and nonfiction. These books help us take the words of Scripture, which were written thousands of years ago, at their meaning in a contemporary context.

The *Hole In Our Gospel* made the point that in recent decades the church in the West has lost sight of the social dimension of the Gospel. The words of grace need to be clothed in the deeds of grace and love if they are to be rightly understood. The way

Jesus put it: "By this all men will know that you are my disciples, if you love one another" (John 13:35). Jesus also said:

> *Come you who are blessed by my Father; take your inheritance, the kingdom prepared for you since the creation of the world. For I was hungry and you gave me something to eat, I was thirsty and you gave me something to drink, I was a stranger, and you invited me in, I needed clothes and you clothed me, I was sick and you looked after me. I was in prison and you came to visit me.*
>
> *Then the righteous will answer him, "Lord, when did we see you hungry, and feed you, or thirsty and give you something to drink? When did we see you a stranger and invite you in, or needing clothes and clothe you? When did we see you sick or in prison and go to visit you?" The King will reply, I tell you the truth, whatever you did for one of the least of these brothers of mine, you did for me. (Matthew 25:34–40)*

Another book that has meant a lot to me is *Evangelism as a Lifestyle* by Jim Petersen. It made the case that evangelism makes much more sense to people when they see it clothed in acts of mercy. He is not preaching the social Gospel, where the acts of mercy are themselves the Gospel. Rather, an understanding of the death, burial, and resurrection of Jesus Christ is best understood in the context of acts of mercy.

> Radical hospitality is all about clothing the Gospel of Jesus Christ in acts of mercy.

The third book is *Open Heart, Open Home* by Karen Burton Mains. I read this book years ago, and it inspired me as I thought through the specifics of this ministry of heartfelt hospitality. One thought-provoking insight is that we all must examine our motives. Are we involved in this ministry to serve or to impress? If we think that everything must be just right, it is possible that our motives are rooted in pride more than we may realize?

Karen also said that we should never clean before company arrives. I found this to be a second intriguing insight. She did not mean that we should never clean but that we should follow a regular cleaning schedule. This keeps us from missing opportunities to serve those who God brings our way. If an opportunity comes to serve when our homes are not tip-top, so be it. We still minister. And if we don't, perhaps that has more to do with our pride than it does with love.

Another of Karen's insights is that we should use all help that comes our way. Whenever someone says: "Is there anything that I can do to help you?" Always say Yes! Heartfelt hospitality is performed best with many hands doing many things. And, if someone wants to help in the kitchen, let him or her help. Some of the best and most meaningful conversations take place as we work together preparing some dish or cleaning up after a meal. It is here where people, especially women, let down their guard and open up.

> **MEDITATION**
> God works when his people pray.

Chapter Fourteen

1. Who was taking the risk: Paul, Evelyn, and Angel in leaving Africa, or Ken and Jane in welcoming complete strangers to their home?

2. Can a Christian trust someone by merely praying with that person on the phone? Can you correctly discern his or her character?

3. Sacrifices are part of the Christian faith. What sacrifices are you making due to your faith?

4. Paul has a goal of returning to Africa and building an orphanage. Do you have goals that affect lives for eternity?

5. Prayer is the best avenue to accomplish God's purpose in our lives. How are you using God's command to pray without ceasing? (Thessalonians 5:17)

Chapter Fifteen

THE NEXT STEP

"Who else," I asked the Lord, "is in need of your tender care, other than the children and the orphans? Where else can the ministry of radical hospitality make a difference?" Again, the Lord provided an answer for me through his Word. James 1:27, which I have quoted previously in this book, "Religion that our Father accepts as pure and faultless is this: to look after orphans and widows in their distress."

This verse had already challenged me in my ministry to orphans. But I had overlooked the needs of widows. As I read and reread this verse, I wondered whether it was possible to interpret the word *widows* to include single mothers—those who no longer have husbands due to divorce. Like widows, single mothers are lacking the spiritual covering of their husbands. By this I mean there is no umbrella of protection or guidance where the single mother can go to seek refuge. In many cases, their divorces were not their choice. I concluded that, indeed, single mothers could be understood to be widows in a broadly framed definition of the word.

I knew we had some single mothers in my church, and hundreds or perhaps thousands lived in my community. Since many of them did not know the Lord, a ministry to single mothers would also be a tool of evangelism.

Prompted by the Holy Spirit, I decided to start a ministry to single mothers. I wondered what to call it and how to get started. God tells us to dream dreams and envision visions (Joel 2:28). I love laying my fleece before God and seeing how he leads. During the first year, Ken and I financed the new ministry to single moms. We imagined what God would do if we just opened our hearts to these overlooked women in our community.

We started small with about fifteen women and had a picnic outside on the church patio one autumn afternoon. Most of the women who attended were from my church. I gave them our ministry brochure with a list of speakers. Laura suggested that we call our ministry SHE, for Sisters Helping Each Other.

God gave me one special partner, Melody, to help start this ministry. We met every few weeks and bathed this ministry with prayer. Before long, the ministry grew to twenty single mothers, with many of these new single mothers coming from outside our church. By the end of the second year, we had an additional forty single mothers. And by the end of the third year, the ministry expanded to two hundred mothers.

Thirteen women now participate with me on the steering committee of this quickly growing ministry.

In addition, Anna serves as our public relations person. The committee helps speakers, events, food, and communications

The exciting part of this ministry is seeing the single mothers networking among themselves and becoming good friends. Even more fulfilling is seeing their desire to become devoted followers of the Lord Jesus Christ. Some of them have joined our church and have had their children baptized.

Background Information about the Single Mothers Ministry

Eve, one of our volunteers decorates the tables attractively and appropriately for each season. She goes garage sale hunting in the summer and finds the best deals and then makes a centerpiece for each of the thirteen tables. At the end of each meeting, the mothers can take them home and place them in their home or apartment. Eve makes Sisters Helping Each Other a pleasant place for women to attend.

A host at each table introduces the ladies and children to each other. A printout sheet of resources is passed out to everyone, as well as an attendance sheet. Everyone's name and address is provided so that the single mothers can all stay in touch with each other. We also have a sheet for prayer requests and dates for the mothers' birthdays, so we can remember them on their special day.

Spa Day is a favorite activity. The ladies are pampered with a shoulder massage, get their nails done, and do other fun activities. We distribute children's clothes in October before the winter season hits in Chicago and again in April before summer begins. In December we host a Christmas party where single mothers are able to choose donated Christmas gifts for their children. We also play a white elephant game that everyone loves, and of course there is always a Christmas message.

In order for readers to appreciate this ministry and the challenges that it can bring to a group, I have included below a few true-life stories of the struggles of being a single mom. Only the names have been changed.

JULIE

Julie is a beautiful, outgoing girl. We enfolded her and her daughters into our family holidays, including Easter and Thanksgiving. One of her daughters stayed at our home three nights a week while Julie completed one of her classes at college.

We fell in love with Julie's daughter who was five years old. We introduced her to all kinds of new food, and she learned to eat them all. At bedtime, we picked out books that had a continuous theme, so she always anticipated the next chapter. Moments after we started reading, she would fall sound asleep until Julie woke her up to take her to her apartment for the remainder of the night.

Reaching out to the children of single moms is a real privilege.

KATRINA

Katrina's parents were from Puerto Rico. A friend of mine suggested Katrina come to our single mothers support group. She came because she was looking for fellowship, and she also wanted to meet other moms who were single.

But nobody could totally identify with Katrina's situation. She privately told me that in three weeks she would be evicted from her current home. She had no place to go. I knew that she worked as a teacher's aide and had two children, a son in seventh grade and a daughter in first grade.

She was a widow, and both of her parents had passed away. She had had thirteen cancer-related surgeries and one heart attack. Finances were enormously limited, and her credit card was maxed out.

Katrina's son told us how the other teachers at school ridiculed her because she did not have a coat to wear while on recess duty. In the bitter cold, she wore a heavy sweater. One day, she worked up enough courage to ask another teacher if she could borrow her coat because the temperatures were down to one-digit frigid levels. The teacher allowed her to borrow the coat but threw it away after Katrina returned it.

Why? This happened just because Katrina was a poor Puerto Rican. I was appalled when I heard this It was hard for me to believe that racial issues existed to this extent in my town. The next Saturday, I took her and her children to a local department store and bought clothes for the family, including a coat for Katrina.

Katrina was now living in a different apartment but still in need of a reliable vehicle. God provided a safe and adequate car for her from a church member's neighbor. God frequently meets the needs of our single moms. Katrina attends our church and her faith remains strong.

JENNIFER

Jennifer is born in the United States, but she married and divorced Henry, who was from Ghana, West Africa. Though Muslim, she did not embrace her Islamic faith. One day she looked on the Internet and found our church and decided to give it a try. She was warmly welcomed into our fellowship and was searching for the truth found in the Bible.

Her eyes were opened and her heart was touched when she read the Bible at Bible study. Because she was a single mother, she decided to come to the SHE ministry.

We loved her and enfolded her into the single mothers group. Once she received Christ as her Savior, she left her boyfriend with whom she had a child, because she knew that he was not an honorable man, and he would not live according to the Word of God. As a result she was homeless, and jobless. Even shelters would not take her because they are not equipped with cribs and there was a waiting list.

On April 18, 2012, Jennifer said, "I chose to obey the Lord and acknowledge him in everything." This meant leaving past relationships behind. Jennifer said, "I am going to submit to God and not man."

My instinct was to bring Jennifer to my home. But my husband, Ken, was hesitant. He agreed to pay for a motel for her. The following night I was very restless, not knowing where Jennifer was sleeping. Ken agreed I could call her. I knew her well because of our interactions at church. I called and found out that she was riding in her car in the city of Chicago with her baby and two children from her previous husband. My heart went out to her. I told her that if she could meet me in our church parking lot by 10:15 p.m., they could stay overnight at our home. It was 9:30 p.m., and she agreed. We met in the church parking lot. She followed me home. All of their belongs were in a black plastic bag. I fed them. They showered and soon were off to sleep in a warm bed. Other friends took them in and they found equipped shelter to help.

Jennifer is still faithfully attending our single mothers support group, where friendships have formed. To this family, we are known as Uncle Ken and Aunt Jane.

Anne

Anne grew up in Pakistan. She questioned the Muslim faith because in her experience all that the leaders in the Muslim religion talked about was their wealth and homes.

Anne was searching for who the Son of God.

When she was a single mom, a window salesman came to her house to repair a window. Somehow they got on the topic of religion and she asked him whom the Son of God was. He said, "Come to a Bible study that meets at our church tonight, and you will find the answer to this question."

She eagerly went to the Bible study and found her answers. She is now a most excited Christian for the Lord and is so willing to share her newfound faith. But she paid a price by admitting she was a born-again Christian. There now is a strained relationship between Anne and her parents. She is afraid to let the rest of her family know she is a Christian because of the shame her parents would feel.

One December morning, Anne heard Moody Radio announce a single mothers ministry at ECRC. She knew this was God answering her prayer for fellowship. She came in as a quiet observer. She was amazed at the fellowship that we all enjoyed.

The following week, I invited her over with another single mom for dinner. We all shared what the Lord was doing in our lives. This was an exciting moment for Anne to actually be invited with her children into another Christian's home to share a meal. We formed a bond, and we are sisters in Christ. Now we have another niece and nephew.

There are so many stories that I could share, and I'm just scratching the surface.

Additional stories that have touched my heart include:

- abandoned children;
- a mother who accidentally took an overdose of her medicine and died in her sleep, leaving behind a fifteen-year-old son with her seventy-year-old grandparents;
- mothers abandoned and left without child support;
- a mother devastated because a father forced his sons to lie under oath for his financial gain;
- mothers who lost their self-esteem due to abuse;
- homeless mothers who live in shelters for a couple of months and then when their time limit is up, find themselves on the streets;
- mothers who are not able to get jobs and provide for their families; and
- mothers who need to be hospitalized due to emotional trauma and cannot afford it.

Through all of these events, I see what an unjust world we are living in. And then I ask myself: "What can be done to change it?" Each person needs to extend a hand of love and concern to needy people in the name of Christ.

God desires to take us all away from the ordinariness of life and plunge us into the realm of the extraordinary. And when God does this, he takes us away from the certainties and securities of life and into the realm of uncertainty. "We live by faith, not by sight," said the Apostle Paul (2 Corinthians 5:7).

As I ventured into the world of unwed mothers and became involved in their real-life stories, there are many that broke my heart. Their problems were so complicated they would sometimes take my breath away.

Would Jesus turn these people away? During his ministry in Palestine, he often directed his attention to the marginalized peoples of society—the prostitutes, the widows, and those deemed unclean for one reason or another. The woman at the well had been married five previous times and was now living in adultery.

So we are called upon to live extraordinary lives. But then, upon deeper reflection, such lives are not so extraordinary. From God's point of view, I think such lives are rather ordinary. Nothing is truly extraordinary about people who live according to the words of Jesus. Such lives are the most normal way for anyone to live.

If we allow our fears or uncertainties to control our lives, we suppress the promptings of the Holy Spirit. Our lives fall short of that sense of divine normalcy and naturalness that God wishes for us all.

But we can't understand this by merely reading a book, or even by merely reading the Bible, for that matter. We have to step out with acts of obedience into the world that God has called us to enter and then walk by faith.

MEDITATION
Follow God's example, therefore, as dearly loved children and walk in the way of love, just as Christ loved us and gave himself up for us as a fragrant offering and sacrifice to God" (Eph. 5:1–2).

Questions for Personal Reflection or Group Discussion

1. Do you know a single mother? If so, does she need assistance? How could you assist her?

2. Are you familiar with what is available in your community to help single moms, such as food pantries, human resources in the county, places like pregnancy assistance centers, counseling resources, housing assistance, financial services, legal services, and shelters?

3. Emotional and spiritual support play a large role in enabling a single mother to become whole again. What can you do with the help of others in your community to provide support groups for such a large segment of our population?

4. Single mothers need to know that they are not alone in this world. What can be done to give them a sense of community?

5. Do you include single mothers in social functions with families or holiday settings? How would this impact your holidays?

6. After hearing the true stories of the individuals in this last chapter, how does this impact your life?

"Therefore, as we have opportunity, let us do good to all people…" (Gal. 6:10).

Conclusion

The great temptation we face in our world today is not to hate God but to gradually ignore him until he is no longer relevant to our lives. Similarly, the second great temptation that we face is not to hate people but to ignore them until they fade from view.

This is precisely what we must not do. Dietrich Bonhoeffer once wrote: "We must be ready to allow ourselves to be interrupted by God, who will thwart our plan and frustrate our ways time and again, even daily, by sending people across our path with their demands and requests."[14]

Bonhoeffer added:

We can then pass them by preoccupied with our more important daily tasks, just as the priest—perhaps reading the Bible—passed by the man who had fallen among robbers...It is strange thing that, of all people, Christians and theologians often consider their work so important and urgent that they do not want to let anything interrupt it. And when we do that, we despise God's crooked yet straight path."[15]

We must never forget that loving God and loving people are intertwined. The Apostle John wrote: "For whoever does not love their brother or sister, whom they have seen, cannot love God whom they have not seen. And he has given us this command: 'Anyone who loves God must also love their brother and sister' (1 John 4:20–21).

A third great temptation facing Christians today is to spiritualize the Christian faith to the point where they reduce its truths to bland generalizations. This lukewarm faith is a world where concrete commands found in Scripture are transformed into vague attitudes detached from practical application. The Bible, which they treasure in their own strange way, fails to challenge and provoke. Those drawn into this third temptation think they are fine, but they are little more than Laodicean Christians, blinded to their own hypocrisies and idolatries.

Just in case you don't know who the Laodicean Christians were, I encourage you to read Revelation 3:14–22. Many pastors have proclaimed in sermons that the church of today, especially the church in the West, is patterned after this troubled first-century church located in the city of Laodicea. Laodicea is nothing but ruins today, a fitting symbol of this kind of Christianity.

We all struggle with these three great temptations. I am first to admit that yielding to them is easy indeed. By nature we are all self-centered. Looking out for "number one" seems to make perfect sense, and we have a world around us that reinforces that message.

What joy it is to see these temptations for what they are and commit ourselves to break free, with the help of the Spirit of God. By sharing a number of my own stories in this book, it is my prayer that the Spirit of God will inspire you to venture forward on your own personal journey where the Word of God is taken seriously—radically so. May you replace the three great temptations in your life with the Two Great Commandments spoken by Jesus.

We must all remind ourselves: the abundant life Jesus promised ("I am come that they might have life, and that they might have it more abundantly," in John 10:10, KJV) is available only to those who take the Two Great Commandments seriously.

My life of practicing biblical hospitality has brought countless joys and blessings into my family's life, joys beyond measure. "You anoint my head with oil; my cup overflows" (Ps. 23:5).

I am also first to admit that Christians should always resist the temptation of becoming one-sided and reducing the complexities of life to simple solutions. Showing forth the love of God in this world in a manner that stresses holiness, avoids the urge of simply throwing money at problems, and strives toward long-term solutions is indeed complicated. Yet, the first step is always obedience to God. The Spirit of God never reveals his hidden work in the lives of people to us. Our responsibility is to join into his work and allow him to carry us alone, never fully understanding what that hidden work happens to be.

In each of the chapters of this book, I have presented glimpses that the Spirit of God has allowed me to see. It is my deepest desire that Christians around the world will become more dedicated to the work of biblical hospitality.

God's commands provide us a framework of how to order our lives. They release us from the so-called wisdom of self-made plans in resolving problems and from our synthetic version of the abundant life. All of this is vanity. In God's commands, we learn, the strikingly peculiar wisdom of *agape* love—a love that has self-sacrifice as its cornerstone. "For whoever wants to save his life will lose it, but whoever loses his life for me will find it" (Matt. 16:25).

For those not touched by the grace of God, all of this must sound silly and even downright absurd. And to those of us who have been touched by divine grace, it sometimes takes courage and faith to venture forward. It's one thing to think of love as merely not stealing from our neighbor. It's quite another to think of love as being Christ to that neighbor and loving that neighbor in the same way that we love ourselves. It is a question of loving the unlovely. It is the joy of watching God transform them so that Christ is seen in their lives also. I wholeheartedly agree with Joyce Meyer, who writes:

> *Loving people unconditionally is a very big challenge. I would be tempted to say it is impossible, but since God tells us to do it, and he never commands us to do something and then leaves to perform it on our own. His grace (his power, ability, and favor) is sufficient for us, which means He enables us to do what He called us to do. God actually sends some people into our lives to function as "sandpaper" to help smooth our rough edges. Learning to walk in love with unlovely people is one of the most important tools God uses to develop our spiritual maturity.*[16]

The road I traveled as I sought to be God's instrument in this important ministry of biblical hospitality may not be yours. God does not make cookie-cutter Christians. But similarities will exist. I trust that each of the fourteen stories presented in this book will spark insights and motivate you to take the first step… and then a second…and then a third.

Make no mistake about it. The world is watching us to see if our walk indeed matches our talk!

Endnotes

1. Anne Graham Lotz, *The Magnificent Obsession: Embracing the God-Filled Life* (Grand Rapids: Zondervan, 2009), 286.
2. Lotz, *My Heart's Cry: Longing for More of Jesus* (Nashville: Thomas Nelson, 2002), 13.
3. Lysa TerKeurst, *What Happens When Women Say Yes to God* (Eugene, Oregon: Harvest House, 2007), 11.
4. Keith A. Sherlin, "Hallmarks of a Godly Marriage," www.essentialchristianity.com.
5. Donna Otto, *Finding Your Purpose as a Mom: How to Build Your Home on Holy Ground* (Eugene, Oregon: Harvest House, 2004), 29.
6. Kay Warren, *Dangerous Surrender: What Happens When You Say Yes to God* (Grand Rapids: Zondervan, 2007), 46.
7. Cited in *Mission Opportunities Short Term: Is It Worth the Risk? (www.mostministries.org/on_field_risks*
8. Dietrich Bonhoeffer, *Life Together* (New York: Harper & Row, 1954), 99.
9. Larry Thompson, *Hidden Heroes* (City: Xulon Press, 2005), 152.
10. Philip Yancey, *Finding God in Unexpected Places* (Colorado Springs: WaterBrook Press, 2005), 147.
11. Ibid., 147, 148.
12. Ibid., 148.
13. Richard Stearns, *The Hole In Our Gospel* (City: Thomas Nelson, 2010), 87.
14. Dietrich Bonhoeffer, Life Together (New York: Harper & Row, 1854, 100
15. Ibid., 100
16. Joyce Meyer, *Love Out Loud* (New York: FaithWords, 2011), 309.

Scripture passages are taken from the New International Version of the Bible, unless it was noted differently by identifying it from the King James Version (KJV).

At the author's request, all royalties from this book will go toward supporting single mothers and the Little Lambs Summer Camps in the Ukraine for orphans.

Jane Loerop
Heartfelt Hospitality

Made in the USA
San Bernardino, CA
09 January 2014